Robert's Rules of Order
Masonic Edition

Revised and Edited by
Michael R. Poll

A Cornerstone Book

Robert's Rules of Order - Masonic Edition
Revised by Michael R. Poll

A Cornerstone Book
Published by Cornerstone Book Publishers

Cornerstone Book Publishers
Hot Springs Village, AR

This work was created and revised from the 1915 Public Domain
Robert's Rules of Order by Henry M. Robert

Seventh Cornerstone Edition - 2023

www.cornerstonepublishers.com

978-1-61342-698-2

Foreword

Simply put, *Robert's Rules of Order* is indispensable for countless clubs and organizations. The logical manner in which proper parliamentary procedure is laid out in this classic work has made it the most accepted and widely used book of its kind. Many clubs and organizations would not consider opening a meeting without a copy of this work within short reach.

Since Masonic lodges operate their meetings within the basic framework of accepted parliamentary procedure, *Robert's Rules of Order* has been the common guide for many lodges. The problem has always been that this work was not written with the Masonic lodge in mind, and Masonic lodges do not always follow classic parliamentary procedures. Many aspects of a properly run lodge are in conflict with what is considered correct parliamentary procedure. An example would be the relationship between the membership of a lodge and the Worshipful Master. In a club, there are times when a membership vote can overturn the presiding officer's ruling. Such is not the case in a Masonic lodge. The nature of the office of Worshipful Master gives the one holding this office authority not held by the presiding officer of most clubs. Any action of the membership of a lodge that infringes on the authority or rights of the Worshipful Master is out of order. This is but one of the conflicts between the classic *Robert's Rule of Order* and the Masonic lodge. While useful and often used in lodges, the classic work must be read with caution as many aspects of the original work do not apply to the lodge.

The Masonic edition of *Robert's Rules of Order* is the classic edition of the work revised and edited with the Masonic lodge in mind. While it has been designed to better follow the general procedures of a well-run business meeting of a lodge, it should not be considered a law book. Nor should anything in this work be considered authoritative when in conflict with an accepted practice within a particular jurisdiction. Each and every Masonic jurisdiction has complete authority over the laws and practices of its lodges, and these may or may not agree with the laws and practices of other jurisdictions. Should anything in this work be found to conflict with the laws or practices of your particular jurisdiction, the conflicting portion of this work should be disregarded.

The Masonic edition of *Robert's Rules of Order* is designed to be a parliamentary guide to a successfully run lodge meeting. The spirit of the work is to aid the Worshipful Master in general parliamentary questions and a valuable educational tool for anyone advancing through the chairs of a lodge.

Michael R. Poll
2005

Contents

Robert's Rules of Order –

Masonic Edition

Art. I

How Business Is Conducted in a Lodge

1. Introduction of Business
2. What Precedes Debate
3. Obtaining the floor
4. Motions and Resolutions
5. Seconding Motions
6. Stating the Question
7. Debate
8. Secondary Motions
9. Putting the Question and Announcing the Vote
10. Proper Motions to Use to Accomplish Certain Objects

1. Introduction of Business.

Business is brought before a lodge either by the motion of a member or by the presentation of a communication to the lodge. It is not usual to make motions to receive reports of committees or communications to the lodge. There are many other cases in the ordinary business routine where the formality of a motion is dispensed with, but should any brother object, a regular motion becomes necessary, or the W. M. may put the question without waiting for a motion.

2. What Precedes Debate.

Before any subject is open to debate, it is necessary, first, that a motion be made by a member of the lodge who has obtained the floor; second, that it be seconded (with certain exceptions); and third, that it be identified as such by the Worshipful Master. The fact that a motion has been made and seconded does not put it before the lodge, as the Worshipful Master alone can do that. He must either rule it out of order or state the question on it so that the lodge may know what is before it for consideration and action, that is, what is the *immediately pending question.* If several questions are pending, such as a resolution and an amendment, and a motion to postpone, the last one stated by the Worshipful Master is the immediately pending question.

While no debate or other motion is in order after a motion is made, until it is stated or ruled out of order by the Worshipful Master, yet brothers may suggest modifications of the motion, and the mover, without the consent of the seconder, has the right to make such modifications as he pleases, or even to withdraw his motion entirely before the Worshipful Master states the question. After it is stated by the W. M., he can do neither without the consent of the lodge, as shown in **27(c)**. A little informal consultation before the question is stated often saves much time, but the Worshipful Master must see that this privilege is not abused and allowed to run into debate. When the mover modifies his motion, the one who seconded it has a right to withdraw his second.

3. Obtaining the Floor.

Before a member can make a motion, or address the lodge in debate, it is necessary that he should *obtain the floor* — that is, he must rise after the floor has been yielded, salute and address the Worshipful Master by his official title, thus, "Worshipful Master," or "Worshipful Brother ..." If the lodge is large so that the brother's name may be unknown to the W. M., the brother should give his name as soon as he catches the eye of the W. M. after addressing him. If the brother is entitled to the floor, as shown hereafter, the W. M. "recognizes" him or assigns him the floor by announcing his name. If the lodge is small and the brothers are known to each other, it is not necessary for the brother to give his name after addressing the W. M., nor is it necessary for the W. M. to do more than bow in recognition of his having the floor. If a brother rises before the floor has been yielded or is standing at the time, he cannot obtain the floor provided anyone else rises afterwards and addresses the WM. It is out of order to be standing when another has the floor, and the one guilty of this violation of the rules cannot claim he rose first, as he did not rise after the floor had been yielded.

Where two or more rise about the same time to claim the floor, all other things being equal, the brother who rose first after the floor had been yielded and addressed the W. M. is entitled to the floor. It frequently occurs, however, that where more than one person claims the floor about the same time, the interests of the lodge require the floor to be assigned to a claimant that was not the first to rise and address the Worshipful Master. There are three classes of such cases that may arise: (1) When a debatable question is immediately pending; (2) when an undebatable question is immediately pending; (3) when no question is pending. In such cases, the W. M. in assigning the floor should be guided by the following principles:

(1) *When a Debatable Question is immediately Pending.* (a) The brother upon whose motion the immediately pending debatable question was brought before the lodge is entitled to be recognized as having the floor (if he has not already spoken on that question) even though another has risen first and addressed the Worshipful Master. The brother thus entitled to preference in recognition in case of a committee's report is the reporting brother (the one who presents or

submits the report); in case of a question taken from the table, it is the one who moved to take the question from the table; in case of the motion to reconsider, it is the one who moved to reconsider, and who is not necessarily the one who calls up the motion. (b) No brother who has already had the floor in debate on the immediately pending question is again entitled to it for debate on the same question. As the interests of the lodge are best served by allowing the floor to alternate between the friends and enemies of a measure, the W. M., when he knows which side of a question is taken by each claimant of the floor, and these claims are not determined by the above principles, should give the preference to the one opposed to the last speaker.

(2) *When an Undebatable Question Is Immediately Pending.* When the immediately pending question is undebatable, its mover has no preference for the floor, which should be assigned in accordance with the principles laid down under (b) in the paragraph below.

(3) *When No Question Is Pending.* (a) When one of a series of motions has been disposed of, and there is no question pending, the next of the series has the right of way, and the W. M. should recognize the brother who introduced the series to make the next motion, even though another has risen first and addressed the Worshipful Master. In fact, no other main motion is in order until the lodge has disposed of the series. Thus, the motion to lay on the table, properly used, is designed to lay aside a question temporarily in order to attend to some more urgent business, and, therefore, if a question is laid on the table, the one who moved to lay it on the table, if he immediately claims the floor, is entitled to it to introduce the urgent business even though another has risen first. So, when the rules are suspended to enable a motion to be made, the mover of the motion to suspend the rules is entitled to the floor to make the motion for which the rules were suspended, even though another rose first. When a brother moves to reconsider a vote for the announced purpose of amending the motion, if the vote is reconsidered, he must be recognized in preference to others in order to move his amendment. (b) If, when no question is pending, and no series of motions has been started that has not been disposed of, a brother rises to move to reconsider a vote or to call up the motion to reconsider that had been previously made, or to take a question from the table when it is in order, he is entitled

4

to the floor in preference to another that may have risen slightly before him to introduce a main motion, provided that when someone rises before him he, on rising, states the purpose for which he rises. If members rising to make the motions mentioned above come into competition, they have the preference in the order in which these motions have just been given; first, to reconsider; and last to take from the table. When a motion to appoint a committee for a certain purpose, or to refer a subject to a committee, has been adopted, no new subject (except a privileged one) can be introduced until the lodge has decided all of the related questions as to the number of the committee, and as to how it shall be appointed, and as to any instructions to be given it. In this case, the one who made the motion to appoint the committee or refer the subject to a committee has no preference in recognition. If he had wished to make the other motions, he should have included them all in his first motion.

From the decision of the W. M. in assigning the floor any two brothers may appeal, one making the appeal and the other seconding it. Where the W. M. is in doubt as to who is entitled to the floor, he may, if he chooses, allow the lodge to decide the question by a vote, the one having the largest vote being entitled to the floor.

If a brother has risen to claim the floor or has been assigned the floor and calls for the question to be made, or it is moved to adjourn or to lay the question on the table, it is the duty of the W. M. to suppress the disorder and protect the brother who is entitled to the floor. A motion cannot be made by one who the W. M. has not recognized as having the floor.

In Order When Another Has the Floor. After a brother has been assigned the floor, he cannot be interrupted by another brother except by (a) a motion to reconsider; (b) a point of order; an objection to the consideration of the question; (d) a call for the orders of the day when they are not being conformed to; (e) a question of privilege; (f) a request or demand that the question be divided when it consists of more than one independent resolution on different subjects; or (g) a parliamentary inquiry or a request for information that requires immediate answer; and these cannot interrupt him after he has commenced speaking unless the urgency is so great as to justify it. The speaker (that is, the brother entitled to the floor) does not lose his right to the floor by these interruptions, and the interrupting brother does not obtain the floor thereby, and after they have been attended to, the W. M. assigns him the floor again. So, when a brother submitting a report from a committee, or offering a resolution, hands it to the secretary to be read, he does not thereby yield his right to the floor. When the reading is finished, and the W. M. states the question, neither the secretary nor anyone else can make a motion until the brother submitting the report, or offering the resolution, has had a reasonable opportunity to claim the floor to which he is entitled, and has not availed himself of his privilege. If, when he submitted the report, he made no motion to accept or adopt the recommendations or resolutions, he should resume the floor as soon as the report is read and make the proper motion to carry out the recommendations, after which he is entitled to the floor for debate as soon as the question is stated.

4. Motions and Resolutions.

A motion is a proposal that the lodge take certain action, or that it expresses itself as holding certain views. It is made by a brother's obtaining the floor as already described and saying, "I move that ..." (which is equivalent to saying, "I propose that"), and then stating the action he proposes to have taken. Thus, a brother "moves" (proposes) that a resolution be adopted, or amended, or referred to a committee, or that a vote of thanks be extended, etc.; or "That it is the sense of this meeting (or lodge) that industrial training," etc. Every resolution should be in writing, and the Worshipful Master has a right to require any main motion, amendment, or instructions to a committee to be in writing. When a main motion is of such importance or length as to be in writing it is usually written in the form of a *resolution*, that is, beginning with the words, "*Resolved*, That," the word "*Resolved*" being underscored (printed in italics) and followed by a comma, and the word "That" beginning with a capital "T." If the word "Resolved" were replaced by the words "I move," the resolution would become a motion. A resolution is always a main motion. In some jurisdictions the word "resolve" may be used instead of "resolution."

When a brother wishes a resolution adopted after having obtained the floor, he says, "I move the adoption of the following resolution," or "I offer the following resolution." In most jurisdictions, a resolution must be submitted in writing and received by the Lodge during a stated meeting and held over, without debate, for a specific period of time in order for due notice to be given to the lodge membership. If it is desired to give the reasons for the resolution, they are usually stated in a *preamble*, each clause of which constitutes a paragraph beginning with "Whereas." The preamble is always amended last, as changes in the resolution may require changes in the preamble. In moving the adoption of a resolution, the preamble is not usually referred to, as it is included in the resolution. But when the previous question is ordered on the resolution before the preamble has been considered for amendment, it does not apply to the preamble, which is then open to debate and amendment. The preamble should never contain a period, but each paragraph should close with a comma or semicolon, followed by "and," except the last paragraph, which should close with the word "therefore," or "therefore, be it." A resolution should avoid periods where practicable. Usually, where periods are necessary, it is better to separate it into a series of resolutions, in which case the resolutions may be numbered, if preferred, by preceding them with the figures 1, 2, etc.; or it may retain the form of a single resolution with several paragraphs, each beginning with "That," and these may be numbered, if preferred, by placing "First," "Second," etc., just before the word "That." The following form will serve as a guide when it is desired to give the reasons for a resolution:

Whereas, The lodge is in need of building repair; and

Whereas, There is not enough funds in the general funds of the lodge; therefore

Resolved, That the annual lodge dues be increased by a sum of $5.00 per Member.

As a general rule, no brother can make two motions at a time except by permission of the Worshipful Master. But he may combine the motion to suspend the rules with the motion for whose adoption it was made; and the motion to reconsider a resolution and its amendments; and a brother may offer a resolution and at the same time move to make it a special order for a specified time.

5. Seconding Motions.

As a general rule, with the exceptions given below, every motion should be seconded. This is to prevent time being consumed in considering a question that only one person favors, and consequently little attention is paid to it in routine motions. Where the W. M. is certain the motion meets with general favor, and yet brothers are slow about seconding it, he may proceed without waiting for a second. Yet, anyone may make a point of order that the motion has not been seconded, and then the W. M. should proceed formally and call for a second. The better way when a motion is not at once seconded, is for the W. M. to ask, "Is the motion seconded?" In a very large hall, the W. M. should repeat the motion before calling for a second in order that all may hear. After a motion has been made no other motion is in order until the W. M. has stated the question on this motion, or has declared, after a reasonable opportunity has been given for a second, that the motion has not been seconded, or has ruled it out of order. Except in very small lodges the W. M. cannot assume that brothers know what the motion is and that it has not been seconded, unless he states the facts.

A motion is seconded by a brother's saying, "I second the motion," or "I second it," which he does without obtaining the floor, and in small lodges without rising. In large lodges, members should rise, and without waiting for recognition, say, "Worshipful Master, I second the motion."

Exceptions.

The following do not require a second:

6. Stating the Question.

When a motion has been made and seconded, it is the duty of the W. M., unless he rules it out of order, immediately to *state the question* — that is, state the exact question that is before the lodge for its consideration and action. This he may do in various ways, depending somewhat on the nature of the question, as illustrated by the following examples: "It is moved and seconded that the following resolution be adopted [reading the resolution];" or "It is moved and seconded to adopt the following resolution;" "Br. A offers the following resolution [read]: the question is on its adoption;" "It is moved and seconded to amend the resolution by striking out the word 'very' before the word 'good';" "The previous question has been demanded [or, moved and seconded] on the amendment;" "It is moved and seconded that the question be laid on the table." If the question is debatable or amendable, the W. M. should immediately ask, "Are you ready for the question?" If no one then rises he should put the question as described in **9**. If the question cannot be debated or amended, he does not ask, "Are you ready for the question?" but immediately puts the question after stating it.

7. Debate.

After a question has been stated by the W. M., it is before the lodge for consideration and action. All resolutions, reports of committees, communications to the lodge, and all amendments proposed to them, and all other motions except the Undebatable Motions mentioned in **45**, may be debated before final action is taken on them, unless by a two-thirds vote the lodge decides to dispose of them without debate. By a two-thirds vote is meant two-thirds of the votes cast. In the debate each brother has the right to speak twice on the same question (except on an appeal) but cannot make a second speech on the same question as long as any brother who has not spoken on that question desires the floor. No one can speak longer than ten minutes at a time without permission of the Worshipful Master.

Debate must be limited to the merits of the *immediately pending question* — that is, the last question stated by the W. M. that is still pending; except that in a few cases the main question is also open to debate [45]. Speakers must address their remarks to the W.M., be courteous in their language and deportment, and avoid all personalities, never alluding to the officers or other brothers by name, where possible to avoid it, nor to the motives of brothers. [For further information on this subject see Debate, 42, and Decorum in Debate, 43.]

8. Secondary Motions.

To assist in the proper disposal of the question various *subsidiary* [12] motions are used, such as to amend, to commit, etc., and for the time being the subsidiary motion replaces the resolution, or motion, and becomes the immediately pending question. While these are pending, a question incidental to the business may arise, as a question of order, and this *incidental* [13] question interrupts the business and, until disposed of, becomes the immediately pending question. And all of these may be superseded by certain motions, called *privileged* [14] motions of such supreme importance as to justify their interrupting all other questions. All of these motions that may be made while the original motion is pending are sometimes referred to as *secondary* motions. The proper use of many of these is shown in 10.

9. Putting the Question and Announcing the Vote.

When the debate appears to have closed, the W. M. asks again, "Are you ready for the question?" If no one rises he proceeds to *put the question* — that is, to take the vote on the question, first calling for the affirmative and then for the negative vote. In putting the question, the W. M. should make perfectly clear what the question is that the lodge is to decide. If the question is on the adoption of a resolution, unless it has been read very recently, it should be read again, the question being put in a way similar to this: "The question is on the adoption of the resolution [which the W. M. reads]; those in favor of the resolution say aye; those opposed say no. The ayes have it, and the resolution is adopted;" or, "The no's have it, and the resolution is lost." Or, thus: "The question is on agreeing to the following resolution," which the W. M. reads, and then he continues, "As many as are in favor of agreeing to the resolution say aye;" after the ayes have responded he continues, "As many as are opposed say no. The ayes have it," etc. Or "It is moved and seconded that an invitation be extended to Br. Jones to address our lodge at its next meeting. Those in favor of the motion will rise; be seated; those opposed will rise. The affirmative has it, and the motion is adopted [or carried]." Or, if the vote is by "show of hands," the question is put, and the vote announced in a form similar to this; "It has been moved and seconded to lay the resolution on the table. Those in favor of the motion will raise the right hand; those opposed will signify [or manifest] it in the same way [or manner]. The affirmative has it [or, The motion is adopted, or carried] and the resolution is laid on the table." The vote should always be announced, as it is a necessary part of putting the question. The lodge is assumed not to know the result of the vote until announced by the W. M., and the vote does not go into effect until announced. As soon as the result of the vote is announced the W. M. should state the next business in order, as in the following example of putting the question on an amendment: "The question is on amending the resolution by inserting the word 'oak' before the word 'desk.' Those in favor of the amendment say aye; those opposed say no. The ayes have it and the amendment is adopted. The question is now [or recurs] on the resolution as amended, which is as follows: [read the resolution as amended]. Are you ready for the question?" The W. M. should never neglect to state what the business is next in order after every vote is announced, nor to state the exact question before the lodge whenever a motion is made. Much confusion is avoided thereby. The vote should always be taken first by the voice or by show of hands (the latter method being often used in small lodges), except in the case of motions requiring a two-thirds vote, when a rising vote should be taken at first. When a division is demanded a rising vote is taken. For further information on voting see **46**. Under each motion is given the form of putting the question whenever the form is peculiar.

10. Proper Motions to Use to Accomplish Certain Objects.

To enable anyone to ascertain what motion to use in order to accomplish what is desired, the common motions are arranged in the table below according to the objects to be attained by their use. Immediately after the table is a brief statement of the differences between the motions placed under each object, and of the circumstances under which each should be used. They include all of the Subsidiary Motions **[12]**, which are designed for properly disposing of a question pending before the lodge; and the three motions designed to again bring before the lodge a question that has been acted upon or laid aside temporarily; and the motion designed to bring before another meeting of the lodge a main question which has been voted on in an unusually small meeting. Motions, as a general rule, require for their adoption only a majority vote — that is, a majority of the votes cast; but motions to suppress or limit debate, or to prevent the consideration of a question, or, without notice to rescind action previously taken, require a two-thirds vote **[48]**. The figures and letters on the left in the list below correspond to similar figures and letters in the statement of differences further on. The figures to the right in the list refer to the sections where the motions are fully treated.

The Common Motions Classified According to Their Objects.

(1) To Modify or Amend.
(a) *Amend* 33
(b) *Commit or Refer* 32
(2) To Defer Action.
(a) *Postpone to a Certain Time* 31
(b) *Make a Special Order* (2/3 Vote)...............20
(c) *Lay on the Table* 28
(3) To Suppress or Limit Debate (2/3 Vote).

(1) *To Modify or Amend.* (a) When a resolution or motion is not worded properly, or requires any modification to meet the approval of the lodge, if the changes required can be made in the lodge, the proper motion to make is to *amend* by "inserting," or "adding," or by "striking out," or by "striking out and inserting," or by "substituting" one or more paragraphs for those in the resolution. (b) But if much time will be required, or if the changes required are numerous, or if additional information is required to enable the lodge to act intelligently, then it is usually better to *refer* the question to a committee.

(2) *To Defer Action.* (a) If it is desired to put off the further consideration of a question to a certain hour, so that when that time arrives, as soon as the pending business is disposed of, it shall have the right of consideration over all questions except special orders and a reconsideration, then the proper motion to make is, *to postpone to that certain time.* This is also the proper motion to make if it is desired to defer action simply to another day. As the motion if adopted cannot interrupt the pending question when the appointed time

arrives, nor can it suspend any rule, it requires only a majority vote for its adoption. A question postponed to a certain time cannot be taken up before the appointed time except by suspending the rules, which requires a two-thirds vote. (b) If it is desired to appoint for the consideration of a question a certain time when it may interrupt any pending question except one relating to adjournment or recess, or a question of privilege or a specified order that was made before it was, then the proper course is to move "that the question be made a *special order* for," etc., specifying the day or hour. As this motion, if adopted, suspends all rules that interfere with the consideration of the question at the appointed time, it requires a two-thirds vote for its adoption. A special order cannot be considered before the appointed time except by suspending the rules, which requires a two-thirds vote. (c) If, however, it is desired to lay the question aside temporarily with the right to take it up at any moment when business of this class, or unfinished or new business, is in order and no other question is before the lodge, the proper motion to use is to *lay the question on the table*. When laid upon the table a majority vote may take it up at the same or the next meeting, as described in **35**.

(3) *To Suppress Debate.* (a) If it is desired to close debate now and bring the lodge at once to a vote on the pending question, or questions, the proper course is to move, or demand, or call for, the previous question on the motions upon which it is desired to close debate. The motion, or demand, for the previous question should always specify the motions upon which it is desired to order the previous question. If no motions are specified, the previous question applies only to the immediately pending question. It requires a two-thirds vote for its adoption. After it has been adopted, privileged and incidental motions may be made, or the pending questions may be laid on the table, but no other subsidiary motion can be made nor is any debate allowed. If it is lost the debate is resumed. (b) If it is desired to limit the number or length of speeches, or the time allowed for debate, the proper course is to move that the speeches or debate be limited as desired, or that the debate be closed, and the vote be taken at a specified time. These motions to limit or close debate require a two-thirds vote for their adoption, and are in order, like the previous question, when any debatable question is immediately pending.

(4) *To Suppress the Question.* A legitimate question cannot be suppressed without free debate, except by a two-thirds vote. If two-thirds of the lodge are opposed to the consideration of the question then it can be suppressed by the following methods: (a) If it is desired to prevent any consideration of the question, the proper course to pursue is *to object to its consideration* before it has been discussed or any other motion stated, and, therefore, it may interrupt a brother who has the floor before the debate has begun. It requires no second. On the question of consideration there must be a two-thirds negative vote to prevent the consideration. (b) After the question has been considered the proper way to immediately suppress it is to close debate by ordering the *previous question,* which requires a two-thirds vote, and then to vote down the question. Another method of suppressing a question is to *postpone it indefinitely* (equivalent to rejecting it), which, however, being debatable and opening the main question to debate, is only of service in giving another opportunity to defeat the resolution should this one fail. For, if the motion to postpone indefinitely is adopted, the main question is dead for that meeting, and if it is lost, the main question is still pending, and its enemies have another opportunity to kill it. When the motion to postpone indefinitely is pending and immediate action is desired, it is necessary to move the previous question as in case (b) above. (d) A fourth method frequently used for suppressing a question is to *lay it on the table,* though this is an unfair use of the motion as otherwise they could not transact business. But in ordinary meetings, where the pressure of business is not so great, it is better policy for the majority to be fair and courteous to the minority and use the proper motions for suppressing a question without allowing full debate, all of which require a two-thirds vote. Unless the enemies of a motion have a large majority, laying it on the table is not a safe way of suppressing it, because its friends, by watching their opportunity, may find themselves in a majority and take it from the table and adopt it, as shown in the next paragraph.

(5) *To Consider a Question a Second Time.* (a) When a question has not been voted on, but has been laid on the table, a majority may *take it from the table* and consider it at any time when no other question is before the lodge and when business of that class, or unfinished or

new business, is in order during the same meeting; or at the next meeting in ordinary societies having regular meetings as often as quarterly. (b) If a motion has been adopted, or rejected, or postponed indefinitely, and afterwards one or more brothers have changed their views from the prevailing to the losing side, and it is thought that by further discussion the lodge may modify or reverse its action, the proper course is for one who voted with the prevailing side to move to *reconsider* the vote on the question. This can be done on the day the vote to be reconsidered is taken, or on the next succeeding day of the same meeting. (c) If a main motion, including questions of privilege and orders of the day, has been adopted, rejected, or postponed indefinitely, and no one is both able and willing to move to reconsider the vote, the question can be brought up again during the same meeting only by moving to *rescind* the motion. To rescind may be moved by any brother, but, if notice of it was not given at a previous meeting, it requires a two-thirds vote or a vote of a majority of the enrolled membership. At any future meeting, the resolution, or other main motion, may be rescinded in the same way if it had been adopted; or it may be introduced anew if it had been rejected or postponed indefinitely; provided the question cannot be reached by calling up the motion to reconsider which had been made at the previous meeting. A bylaw, or anything else that requires a definite notice and vote for its amendment, requires the same notice and vote to rescind it.

(6) *To Prevent Final Action on a Question in an Unusually Small Meeting.* If an important main motion should be adopted, lost, or postponed indefinitely, at a small meeting of the lodge when it was apparent that the action is in opposition to the views of the majority of the brothers, the proper course to pursue is for a brother to vote with the prevailing side and then move to reconsider the vote and have it entered on the minutes. The motion to reconsider, in this form, can be made only on the day the vote was taken which it is proposed to reconsider, and the reconsideration cannot be called up on that day; thus, an opportunity is given to notify absent brothers. The motion to reconsider is fully explained in **36**.

Art. II

General Classification of Motions

11. Main or Principal Motions
12. Subsidiary Motions
13. Incidental Motions
14. Privileged Motions
15. Some Main and Unclassified Motions

11. Main or Principal Motions

A Main (or Principal) motion is one made to bring before the lodge, for its consideration, on any particular subject. It takes precedence of nothing — that is, it cannot be made when any other question is before the lodge; and it yields to all Privileged, Incidental, and Subsidiary Motions — that is, any of these motions can be made while a main motion is pending. Main motions are debatable, and subject to amendment, and can have any subsidiary [12] motions applied to them. When a main motion is laid on the table, or postponed to a certain time, it carries with it all pending subsidiary motions. If a main motion is referred to a committee it carries with it only the pending amendments. As a general rule, they require for their adoption only a majority vote — that is, a majority of the votes cast; but amendments to constitutions, bylaws, and rules of order already adopted, all of which are main motions, require a two-thirds vote for their adoption, unless the bylaws, etc., specify a different vote for their amendment; and the motion to rescind action previously taken requires a two-thirds vote, or a vote of a majority of the entire membership, unless previous notice of the motion has been given.

Main motions may be subdivided into Original Main Motions and Incidental Main Motions. *Original Main Motions* are those which bring before the lodge some new subject, generally in the form of a resolution, upon which action by the lodge is desired. *Incidental Main Motions* are those main motions that are incidental to, or relate to, the business of the lodge, or its past or future action, as, a committee's report on a resolution referred to it. A motion to accept or adopt the report of a standing committee upon a subject not referred to it is an original main motion, but a motion to adopt a report on a subject referred to a committee is an incidental main motion. The introduction of an original main motion can be prevented by sustaining by a two-thirds vote an objection to its consideration [23], made just after the main motion is stated and before it is discussed. An objection to its consideration cannot be applied to an incidental main motion, but a two-thirds vote can immediately suppress it by ordering the previous question [29]. This is the only difference between the two classes of main motions.

The following list contains some of the most common Incidental Main Motions.

Accept or Adopt a Report upon a subject referred to a committee **[54]**
Appoint the Time and Place for a special meeting, if introduced when no business is pending **[16]**
Amend the Bylaws, Standing Rules, or Resolutions, etc., already adopted 66
Ratify or *Confirm* action taken 39
Rescind or *Repeal* action taken 37

All of these motions are essentially main motions, and are treated as such, though they may appear otherwise.

Though a question of privilege is of high rank as far as interrupting a pending question is concerned, yet when the question has interrupted business and is pending, it is treated as a main motion as far as having incidental and subsidiary motions applied to it. So, an order of the day, even though a special order, after it has been taken up is treated in the same way, as is also a question that has been reconsidered.

No motion is in order that conflicts with the constitution, bylaws, or edicts of the lodge or Grand Lodge, and if such a motion is adopted it is null and void. Before introducing such a motion, it is necessary to amend the constitution or bylaws. Since the lodge is subordinate to the Grand Lodge, the Grand Lodge, itself, must change any conflicting rules or laws before a lodge can entertain any motions that are in conflict with any constitution, bylaws, or edicts of the Grand Lodge. So, too, a motion is not in order that conflicts with a resolution previously adopted by the lodge at the same meeting, or that has been introduced and has not been finally disposed of. If it is not too late the proper course is to reconsider **[36]** the vote on the motion previously adopted, and then amend it so as to express the desired idea. If it cannot be reconsidered, then by a two-thirds vote the old resolution may be rescinded when the new one can be introduced, or by giving notice it may be rescinded by a majority vote at the next meeting. In profane societies, where the quorum is a small percentage of the membership, and the meetings are as frequent as quarterly, no resolution that conflicts with one adopted at a previous meeting should be entertained until the old one has been rescinded, which requires a two-thirds vote unless proper notice has been given. [See **37**.]

12. Subsidiary Motions

Subsidiary Motions are such as are applied to other motions for the purpose of most appropriately disposing of them. By means of them the original motion may be modified, or action postponed, or it may be referred to a committee to investigate and report, etc. They may be applied to any main motion, and when made they supersede the main motion and must be decided before the main motion can be acted upon. None of them, except the motion to amend and those that close or limit or extend the limits of debate, can be applied to a subsidiary, incidental (except an appeal in certain cases), or privileged motion. Subsidiary motions, except to lay on the table, the previous question, and postpone indefinitely, may be amended. The motions affecting the limits of debate may be applied to any debatable question regardless of its privilege and require a two-thirds vote for their adoption. All those of lower rank than those affecting the limits of debate are debatable, the rest are not. The motion to amend anything that has already been adopted, as bylaws or minutes, is not a subsidiary motion but is a main motion and can be laid on the table or have applied to it any other subsidiary motion without affecting the bylaws or minutes, because the latter are not pending.

In the following list the subsidiary motions are arranged in the order of their precedence, the first one having the highest rank. When one of them is the immediately pending question every motion above it is in order, and everyone below it is out of order.

They are as follows:

Subsidiary Motions.

13. Incidental Motions

Incidental Motions are such as arise out of another question which is pending, and therefore take precedence of and must be decided before the question out of which they rise; or they are incidental to a question that has just been pending and should be decided before any other business is taken up. They yield to privileged motions, and generally to the motion to lay on the table. They are undebatable, except an appeal under certain circumstances as shown in **21**. They cannot be amended except where they relate to the division of a question, or to the method of considering a question, or to methods of voting, or to the time when nominations shall be closed. No subsidiary motion, except to amend, can be applied to any of them except a debatable appeal. Whenever it is stated that all incidental motions take precedence of a certain motion, the incidental motions referred to are only those that are legitimately incidental at the time they are made. Thus, incidental motions take precedence of subsidiary motions, but the incidental motion to object to the consideration of a question cannot be made while a subsidiary motion is pending, as the objection is only legitimate against an original main motion just after it is stated, before it has been debated, or there has been any subsidiary motion stated. The following list comprises most of those that may arise:

Incidental Motions.

14. Privileged Motions

Privileged Motions are such as, while not relating to the pending question, are of so great importance as to require them to take precedence of all other questions, and, on account of this high privilege, they are undebatable. They cannot have any subsidiary motion applied to them, except the motions to fix the time to which to adjourn, and to take a recess, which may be amended. But after the lodge has actually taken up the orders of the day or a question of privilege, debate and amendment are permitted, and the subsidiary motions may be applied the same as on any main motion. These motions are as follows, being arranged in order of precedence:

Privileged Motions.

15. Some Main and Unclassified Motions.

Two main motions (to rescind and to ratify) and several motions which cannot conveniently be classified as either Main, Subsidiary, Incidental, or Privileged, and which are in common use, are hereafter explained and their privileges and effects given. They are as follows:

Art. III
Privileged Motions

16. Fix the Time to which the Lodge shall Close
17. Close
18. Calling the Lodge to Recess (Refreshment)
19. Questions of Privilege
20. Orders of the Day

16. Fix the Time to which the Lodge shall Close.

The Worshipful Master may, at his pleasure, rule any motion to fix a time to close as out of order. In some cases, the time to close is fixed by the lodge Bylaws. If the W.M. sees fit to entertain a motion to close for some special circumstance, the motion is privileged only when made while another question is pending. If a time to close is fixed by the bylaws, the time set by the motion cannot be beyond that time. If made in a lodge when no question is pending, this is a main motion and may be debated and amended and have applied to it the other subsidiary motions, like other main motions. Whenever the motion is referred to in these rules the privileged motion is meant, unless specified to the contrary.

This motion when privileged takes precedence of all others and is in order even after it has been voted to close. It can be amended, and a vote on it can be reconsidered.

17. Close.

While it is rarely done in a Masonic lodge (and if allowed by the W.M. or G.L. law), a motion to close the lodge is always a privileged motion except when, for lack of provision for a future meeting, as in a mass meeting, or at the last meeting of a convention, its effect, if adopted, would be to dissolve the lodge permanently. When not privileged it is treated as any other main motion, being debatable and amendable, etc.

The privileged motion to close takes precedence of all others, except the privileged motion "to fix the time to which to close," to which it yields. It is not debatable, nor can it be amended or have any other subsidiary [12] motion applied to it; nor can a vote on it be reconsidered. It may be withdrawn.

The motion to close can be repeated if there has been any intervening business, though it is simply progress in debate. The W.M. may decline to close in order to hear one speech or to take one vote, and therefore it must have the privilege of renewing the motion to close when there has been any progress in business or debate. But this high privilege is liable to abuse to the annoyance of the lodge, if the W. M. does not prevent it by refusing to entertain the motion when evidently made for obstructive purposes, as when the lodge has just voted it down, and nothing has occurred since to show the possibility of the lodge's wishing to adjourn. [See Dilatory Motions, **40**.]

The motion to close, like every other motion, cannot be made except by a brother who has the floor. When made by one who has not risen and addressed the W. M. and been recognized, it can be entertained only by general consent. It cannot be made when the lodge is engaged in voting, or verifying the vote, but is in order after the vote has been taken by ballot before it has been announced. In such case the ballot vote should be announced as soon as business is resumed. Where much time will be consumed in counting ballots the W.M. may put the lodge at recess, as explained in the next section. No appeal, or question of order, or inquiry, should be entertained after the motion to close has been made, unless it is of such a nature that its decision is necessary before closing.

Before closing, the W. M., should be sure that no important matters have been overlooked. If there are announcements to be made, they should be attended to before taking the vote, or at least, before announcing it. If there is something requiring action before closing, the fact should be stated, and the mover requested to withdraw his motion to close. The fact that the motion to close is undebatable does not prevent the lodge's being informed of business requiring attention before closing.

An adjournment *sine die* — that is, without day — closes the lodge and if there is no provision for convening the lodge again, the adjournment can dissolve the lodge. This adjournment would be in order only if the lodge were turning in its charter. But, if any provision has been made, or understood, whereby another meeting may be held, its effect is simply to close the lodge.

When the motion to close is qualified in any way, or when its effect is to dissolve the lodge without any provision being made for holding another meeting of the lodge, it loses its privilege and is a main motion, debatable and amendable and subject to having applied to it any of the subsidiary motions.

In committees where no provision has been made for future meetings, an adjournment is always at the call of the chairman unless otherwise specified. When a special committee, or the committee of the whole, has completed the business referred to it, instead of adjourning, it rises and reports, which is equivalent to adjournment without day.

The Effect upon Unfinished Business of a closing, unless the lodge has adopted rules to the contrary, is as follows:

When the closing does not permanently close the lodge, the business interrupted by it is the first in order after the reading of the minutes at the next meeting, and is treated the same as if there had been no closing.

18. Calling the Lodge to Recess (Refreshment).

This motion is practically a combination of the two preceding, to which it yields, taking precedence of all other motions. If made when other business is before the lodge, it is a privileged motion and is undebatable and can have no subsidiary motion applied to it except amend. It can be amended as to the length of the recess. It takes effect immediately. A motion to take a recess made when no business is before the lodge, or a motion to take a recess at a future time, has no privilege, and is treated as any other main motion. A recess is an intermission in the day's proceedings, as for meals or for counting the ballots when much time is required; or in the case of meetings like conventions lasting for several days a recess is sometimes taken over an entire day. When a recess is provided for in the order of exercises, or program, the W. M., when the time arrives, announces the fact, and says the lodge is at recess. When the hour has arrived to which the recess was taken, the W. M. calls the lodge to order, and the business proceeds the same as if no recess had been taken. If the recess was taken after a vote had been taken and before it was announced, then the first business is the announcement of the vote. The intermissions in the proceedings of a day are termed recesses, whether the lodge voted to take a recess, or whether it simply adjourned having previously adopted a program or rule providing for the hours of meeting. The W.M. may put the lodge at refreshment at his will and pleasure. He may also rule out of order any motion to put the lodge at refreshment if he feels that it would better serve the lodge.

19. Questions of Privilege.

Questions relating to the rights and privileges of the lodge, or to any of its members, take precedence of all other motions except any relating to closing and recess, to which they yield. If the question is one requiring immediate action it may interrupt a brother's speech; as, for example, when, from any cause, a report that is being read cannot be heard in a part of the lodge. But if it is not of such urgency, it should not interrupt a brother after he has commenced his speech. Before a brother has commenced speaking, even though he has been assigned the floor, it is in order for another brother to raise a question of privilege. When a brother rises for this purpose, he should not wait to be recognized, but immediately on rising should say, "Worshipful Master," — and when he catches the W. M.'s eye, should add, "I rise to a question of privilege affecting the lodge," or "I rise to a question of personal privilege." The W. M. directs him to state his question and then decides whether it is one of privilege or not. The W. M. may decide it to be a question of privilege, but not of sufficient urgency to justify interrupting the speaker. In such a case the speaker should be allowed to continue, and, when he has finished, the W. M. should immediately assign the floor to the brother who raised the question of privilege to make his motion if one is necessary. Whenever his motion is made and stated, it becomes the immediately pending question and is open to debate and amendment and the application of all the other subsidiary motions just as any main motion. Its high privilege extends only to giving it the right to consideration in preference to any other question except one relating to adjournment or recess, and, in cases of great urgency, the right to interrupt a brother while speaking. It cannot interrupt voting or verifying a vote. As soon as the question of privilege is disposed of, the business is resumed exactly where it was interrupted; if a brother had the floor at the time the question of privilege was raised, the W. M. assigns him the floor again.

Questions of privilege may relate to the privileges of the lodge or only of a brother, the former having the precedence if the two come into competition. Questions of personal privilege must relate to one as a member of the lodge. Questions like the following relate to the privileges of the lodge: those relating to the organization of the lodge; or to the comfort of its members, as the heating, lighting, ventilation, etc., of the hall, and freedom from noise and other disturbance; or to the conduct of its officers; or to the calling to order of a brother for disorderly conduct or other offence; or to the accuracy of published reports of proceedings.

Privileged questions include, besides questions of privilege, a call for the orders of the day and the privileged motions relating to adjournment and recess. This distinction between privileged questions and questions of privilege should be borne in mind.

20. Orders of the Day.

A Call for the Orders of the Day (which, in a regular meeting, is a request that the lodge conform to its program or order of business) can be made at any time when no other privileged [14] motion is pending and the order of business is being varied from, and only then. It requires no second, as a single brother has a right to request that the order of business be conformed to, while the final decision of the order is with the Worshipful Master. It is out of order to call for the orders of the day when there is no variation from the order of business. Thus, the orders of the day cannot be called for when another question is pending, provided there are no special orders made for that time or an earlier time, as general orders cannot interrupt a question actually under consideration. The call must be simply for the orders of the day, and not for a specified one, as the latter has no privilege. When the time has arrived for which a special order has been made, a call for the orders of the day taken precedence of everything except the other privileged motions, namely, those relating to adjournment and recess, and questions of privilege, to which it yields. If there are no special orders a call for the orders of the day cannot interrupt a pending question; but, if made when no question is pending, it is in order provided the W. M. has not stated the question or ruled that he is changing the order of business. Until the time of taking up the general orders for consideration this call yields to a motion to reconsider, or to a calling up of a motion to reconsider, previously made. A call for the orders of the day cannot be debated or amended, or have any other subsidiary motion applied to it.

It is the duty of the W. M. to announce the business to come before the lodge, and if he always performs this duty there will be no occasion for calling for the orders of the day. It must be understood that any call for the orders of the day is a *request* as it is the right and privilege of the W.M. to change the order of business at his will and pleasure.

Orders of the Day. When one or more subjects have been assigned to a particular day or hour (by postponing them to, or making them special orders for, that day or hour, or by adopting a program or order of business), they become the orders of the day for that day or hour, and they should not be considered before that time, except by a two-thirds vote. They are divided into General Orders and Special Orders, the latter always taking precedence of the former.

A *General Order* is usually made by simply postponing a question to a certain day or hour, or after a certain event. It does not suspend any rule, and therefore cannot interrupt business. But after the appointed hour has arrived it has the preference, when no question is pending, over all other questions except special orders and reconsideration. It should not be considered before the appointed time except by a reconsideration or by a two-thirds vote. When the order of business provides for orders of the day, questions simply postponed to a meeting, without specifying the hour, come up under that head. If no provision is made for orders of the day, then such postponed questions come up after the disposal of the business pending at the previous adjournment, and after the questions on the calendar that were not disposed of at the previous meeting.

An order of business that specifies the order in which, but not the time when, the business shall be transacted, together with the postponed questions constitutes the general orders. This order should not be varied from except by general consent or by suspending the rules by a two-thirds vote. If all of this business is not disposed of before adjournment, it becomes "unfinished business," and is treated as unfinished business, as explained in **17**.

As general orders cannot interrupt the consideration of a pending question, it follows that any general order made for an earlier hour, though made afterwards, by not being disposed of in time may interfere with the general order previously made. Therefore, general orders must take precedence among themselves in the order of the times to which they were postponed, regardless of when the general order was made. If several are appointed for the same time, then they take precedence in the order in which they were made. If several appointed for the same time were made at the same time, then they take precedence in the order in which they were arranged in the motion making the general order.

To *Make a Special Order* requires a two-thirds vote, because it suspends all rules that interfere with its consideration at the specific time, except those relating to motions for adjournment or recess, or to questions of privilege or to special orders made before it was made. A pending question is made a special order for a future time by "Postponing it and making it a special order for that time." [See Postpone to a Certain Time, **31**, which should be read in connection with this section.] If the question is not pending, the motion to make it a special order for a certain time is a main motion, debatable, amendable, etc. The brother desirous of making it a special order should obtain the floor when nothing is pending, and business of that class, or new business, is in order, and say, "I move that the following resolution be made the special order for [specifying the time]," and then reads the resolution and hands it to the Worshipful Master. Or he may adopt this form: "I offer the following resolution, and move that it be made a special order for the next meeting." Or, in case a committee has been appointed to submit a revision of the constitution, the following resolution may be adopted: "Resolved, That the revision of the constitution be made the special order for Thursday evening and thereafter until it is disposed of." Another way of making special orders is by adopting a program, or order of business, in which is specified the hour for taking up each topic.

Program. It is customary to adopt a program, or order of business, in conventions in meeting for several days (this would normally not be a lodge meeting). Since the delegates and invited speakers come from a distance, it is very important that the program be strictly adhered to. No change can be made in it after its adoption by the body, except by a two-thirds vote. When the hour assigned to a certain topic arrives, the W. M. (or presiding officer) puts to vote any questions pending and announces the topic for the hour. This is done because, under such circumstances, the form of the program implies that the hour, or other time, assigned to each topic is all that can be allowed. But, if anyone moves to lay the question on the table, or postpone it to a certain time, or refer it to a committee, the W. M. should recognize the motion and immediately put it to vote without debate. Should any one move to extend the time allotted the pending question, it should be decided instantly without debate, a two-thirds vote being necessary for the extension. It is seldom that an extension is desirable, as it is unfair to the next topic. When an invited speaker exceeds his time, it is extremely discourteous to call for the orders of the day. The presiding officer should have an understanding with invited speakers as to how he will indicate the expiration of their time. This can be done by tapping on a book or a bell. It is usually better to have it understood that the signal will be given one minute before the time expires, or longer if the speaker wishes it, so that he can properly close his address.

A series of special orders made by a single vote is treated the same as a program — that is, at the hour assigned to a particular subject it interrupts the question assigned to the previous hour. If it is desired to continue the discussion of the pending topic at another time, it can be laid on the table or postponed until after the close of the interrupting question, by a majority vote.

Special Orders made at different times for specified hours. When special orders that have been made at different times come into conflict, the one that was first made takes precedence of all special orders made afterwards, though the latter were made for an earlier hour. No special order can be made so as to interfere with one previously made. By reconsidering the vote making the first special order, they can be arranged in the order desired. Suppose after a special order has been made for 7:30 P.M., one is made for 7:15 P.M., and still later one is made for 8 P.M.; if the 7:15 P.M. order is pending at 7:30 P.M., the order for 7:30 P.M., having been made first, interrupts it and continues, if not previously disposed of, beyond 8 P.M., regardless of the special order for that hour. When it, the 7:30 P.M. order, is disposed of, the special order for 7:15 P.M. is resumed even if it is after 8 o'clock, because the 7:15 P.M. order was made before the 8 P.M. order. The only exception to this rule is in the case of the hour fixed for recess or closing of the lodge. When that hour arrives the W. M. announces it and closes the lodge, or puts it at recess, even though there is a special order pending that was made before the hour for recess or closing was fixed. When the W. M. announces the hour, anyone can request to postpone the time for closing, or to extend the time for considering the pending question a certain number of minutes.

Special Orders when only the day or meeting is specified. Often subjects are made special orders for a meeting without specifying an hour. If the order of business provides for orders of the day, they come up under that head, taking precedence of general orders. If there is no provision for orders of the day, they come up under unfinished business — that is, before new business. If there is no order of business, then they may be called up at any time after the minutes are disposed of.

The Special Order for a Meeting. Sometimes a subject is made the special order for a meeting in which case it is announced by the W. M. as the pending business immediately after the disposal of the minutes. This particular form is used when it is desired to devote an entire meeting, or so much of it as is necessary, to considering a special subject, as the revision of the bylaws. This form of a special order should take precedence of the other forms of special orders. It is debatable and amendable.

Art. IV

Incidental Motions

21. Questions of Order and Appeal.

A *Question of Order* takes precedence of the pending question out of which it arises; is in order when another has the floor, even interrupting a speech or the reading of a report; does not require a second; cannot be amended or have any other subsidiary motion applied to it; yields to privileged motions and the motion to lay on the table; and must be decided by the W.M. without debate, unless in doubtful cases he submits the question to the lodge for decision, in which case it is debatable whenever an appeal would be. Before rendering his decision, he may request the advice of brothers of experience, which advice or opinion should usually be given sitting to avoid the appearance of debate. If the W. M. is still in doubt, he may submit the question to the lodge for its decision in a manner similar to this: "Br. A raises the point of order that the amendment just offered [state the amendment] is not germane to the resolution. The W. M. is in doubt, and submits the question to the lodge. The question is, 'Is the amendment germane to the resolution?'" As no appeal can be taken from the decision of the lodge (Grand Lodge excepted), this question is open to debate whenever an appeal would be, if the W. M. decided the question and an appeal were made from that decision. Therefore, it is debatable except when it relates to indecorum, or transgression of the rules of speaking, or to the priority of business, or when it is made during a division of the lodge, or while an undebatable question is pending. The question is put thus: "As many as are of opinion that the amendment is germane [or that the point is well taken] say aye; as many as are of a contrary opinion say no. The ayes have it, the amendment is in order, and the question is on its adoption." If the negative vote is the larger it would be announced thus: "The no's have it, the amendment is out of order, and the question is on the adoption of the resolution." Whenever the W.M. decides a question of order, he has the right, if he chooses, to state the reasons for his decision, but there is no right of appeal of the decision by the membership of the lodge.

It is the duty of the W.M. to enforce the rules and orders of the lodge, without debate or delay. It is also the right of every brother who notices the breach of a rule, to request its enforcement. In such a case he rises from his seat and says, "W. M., I rise to a point of order."

The speaker immediately takes his seat, and the W. M. requests the brother to state his point of order, which he does and resumes his seat. The W. M. decides the point, and then, if the brother has not been guilty of any serious breach of decorum, the W. M. permits him to resume his speech. But, if his remarks are decided to be improper and anyone objects, he cannot continue without a ruling from the Worshipful Master. [See **43** for a full treatment of this subject of indecorum in debate]. The question of order must be raised at the time the breach of order occurs, so that after a motion has been discussed it is too late to raise the question as to whether it was in order, or for the W. M. to rule the motion out of order. The only exception is where the motion is in violation of the laws, or the constitution, bylaws, or standing rules of the lodge or Grand Lodge, or of fundamental parliamentary principles, so that if adopted it would be null and void. In such cases it is never too late to raise a point of order against the motion. This is called raising a question, or point, of order, because the brother in effect puts to the W. M., whose duty it is to enforce order, the question as to whether there is not now a breach of order.

Instead of the method just described, it is usual, when it is simply a case of improper language used in debate, for the W. M. to call the speaker to order, or for a brother to say, "I call the brother to order." The W. M. decides whether the speaker is in or out of order, and proceeds as before.

Appeal. There is no appeal from any decision of the Worshipful Master. Unlike many non-Masonic organizations, a decision made by the W.M. is only reversible by the Grand Lodge or Grand Master, if it is found to be in violation of any lodge or Grand Lodge law.

22. Suspension of the Rules.

A motion to suspend the rules is rarely in order in a Masonic lodge. If in order, the motion to suspend the rules may be made when no question is pending; or while a question is pending, provided it is for a purpose connected with that question. It yields to all the privileged motions (except a call for the orders of the day), to the motion to lay on the table, and to incidental motions arising out of itself. It is undebatable and cannot be amended or have any other subsidiary motion applied to it, nor can a vote on it be reconsidered, nor can a motion to suspend the rules for the same purpose be renewed at the same meeting except by unanimous consent, though it may be renewed after an adjournment, even if the next meeting is held the same day.

When the lodge wishes to do something that cannot be done without violating its own rules, and yet it is not in conflict with the constitution, or bylaws of the lodge or Grand Lodge, or with the fundamental principles of parliamentary law, it "suspends the rules that interfere with" the proposed action. The object of the suspension must be specified, and nothing else can be done under the suspension. The rules that can be suspended are those relating to priority of business, or to business procedure, etc., and would usually be comprised under the heads of rules of order. Sometimes lodges include in their bylaws rules relating to the transaction of business without any intention, evidently, of giving these rules any greater stability than is possessed by other rules of their class, and they may be suspended the same as if they were called rules of order. A standing rule as defined in **65** may be suspended by a majority vote. But sometimes the term "standing rules" is applied to what are strictly rules of order, and then, like rules of order, they require a two-thirds vote for their suspension. Nothing that requires previous notice, and a two-thirds vote for its amendment can be suspended by less than a two-thirds vote.

No rule can be suspended when the negative vote is as large as the minority protected by that rule; nor can a rule protecting absentees be suspended even by general consent or a unanimous vote. For instance, a rule requiring notice of a motion to be given at a previous meeting cannot be suspended by a unanimous vote, as it protects absentees who do not give their consent. A rule requiring officers to be elected by ballot cannot be suspended by a unanimous vote, because the rule protects a minority of one from exposing his vote, and this he must do if he votes openly in the negative, or objects to giving general consent. If it is desired to allow the suspension of a by-law that cannot be suspended under these rules, then it is necessary to provide in the bylaws for its suspension.

The *Form* of this motion is, "to suspend the rules that interfere with," etc., stating the object of the suspension, as, "the consideration of a resolution on ....," which resolution is immediately offered after the rules are suspended, the W. M. recognizing for that purpose the brother that moved to suspend the rules, or, if it is desired to consider a question which has been laid on the table, and cannot be taken up at that time because that class of business is not then in order, or to consider a question that has been postponed to another time, or that is in the order of business for another time, then the motion may be made thus, "I move to suspend the rules and take up [or consider] the resolution ......" When the object is not to take up a question for discussion but to adopt it without debate, the motion is made thus: "I move to suspend the rules and adopt [or agree to] the following resolution," which is then read: or, "I move to suspend the rules, and adopt [or agree to] the resolution on ..." The same form may be used in a case like this: "I move to suspend the rules, and admit to the privileges of the floor brothers of sister societies," which merely admits them to the hall.

Instead of a formal motion to suspend the rules, it is more usual to ask for general consent to do the particular business that is out of order. As soon as the request is made the W. M. inquires if there is any objection, and if no one objects, he directs the brother to proceed just as if the rules had been suspended by a formal vote. [See General Consent **48**.]

23. Objection to the Consideration of a Question.

An objection may be made to the consideration of any original main motion, and to no others, provided it is made before there is any debate or before any subsidiary motion is stated. Thus, it may be applied to petitions and to communications that are not from the Grand Lodge, as well as to resolutions. It cannot be applied to incidental main motions [**11**], such as amendments to bylaws, or to reports of committees on subjects referred to them, etc. It is similar to a question of order in that it can be made when another has the floor, and does not require a second; and as the W. M. can call a brother to order, so he can put this question, if he deems it advisable, upon his own responsibility. It cannot be debated, or amended, or have any other subsidiary motion applied to it. It yields to privileged motions and to the motion to lay on the table. A negative, but not an affirmative vote on the consideration may be reconsidered.

When an original main motion is made and any brother wishes to prevent its consideration, he rises, although another has the floor, and says, "W. M., I object to its consideration." The W. M. immediately puts the question, "The consideration of the question has been objected to: Will the lodge consider it? [or, Shall the question be considered?]" If decided in the negative by a two-thirds vote, the whole matter is dismissed for that meeting; otherwise, the discussion continues as if this objection had never been made. The same question may be introduced at any succeeding meeting.

The *Object* of this motion is not to cut off debate (for which other motions are provided) but to enable the lodge to avoid altogether any question which it may deem irrelevant, unprofitable, or contentious. If the W. M. considers the question entirely outside the objects of the lodge, he should rule it out of order, from which decision no appeal may be taken.

Objection to the consideration of a question must not be confounded with objecting where unanimous consent, or a majority vote, is required. Thus, in case of the minority of a committee desiring to submit their views, a single brother saying, "I object," prevents it, unless the lodge by a majority vote grants them permission.

24. Division of a Question, and Consideration by Paragraph.

Division of a Question. The motion to divide a question can be applied only to main motions and to amendments. It takes precedence of nothing but the motion to postpone indefinitely, and yields to all privileged, incidental, and subsidiary motions except to amend and to postpone indefinitely. It may be amended but can have no other subsidiary motion applied to it. It is undebatable. It may be made at any time when the question to be divided, or the motion to postpone indefinitely, is immediately pending, even after the previous question has been ordered. But it is preferable to divide the question when it is first introduced. When divided each resolution or proposition is considered and voted on separately, the same as if it had been offered alone. The motion to adopt, which was pending when the question was divided, applies to all the parts into which the question has been divided and should not, therefore, be repeated. The formality of a vote on dividing the question is generally dispensed with, as it is usually arranged by general consent. But if this cannot be done, then a formal motion to divide is necessary, specifying the exact method of division.

When a motion relating to a certain subject contains several parts, each of which is capable of standing as a complete proposition if the others are removed, it can be divided into two or more propositions to be considered and voted on as distinct questions, by the lodge's adopting a motion to divide the question in a specified manner. The motion must clearly state how the question is to be divided, and anyone else may propose a different division, and these different propositions, or amendments, should be treated as filling blanks; that is, they should be voted on in the order in which they are made, unless they suggest different numbers of questions, when the largest number is voted on first. If a resolution includes several distinct propositions, but is so written that they cannot be separated without its being rewritten, the question cannot be divided. The division must not require the secretary to do more than to mechanically separate the resolution into the required parts, prefixing to each part the words "*Resolved*, That," or "*Ordered*, That," and dropping conjunctions when necessary, and replacing pronouns by the nouns for which they stand, wherever the division makes it necessary. When the question is decided, each separate question must be a proper one for the lodge to act upon, if none of the others is adopted. Thus, a motion to "commit with instructions" is indivisible; because, if divided, and the motion to commit should fail, then the other motion, to instruct the committee, would be absurd, as there would be no committee to instruct. The motion to "strike out certain words and insert others" is strictly one proposition and therefore indivisible.

If a series of independent resolutions relating to different subjects is included in one motion, it must be divided on the request of a single brother, which request may be made while another has the floor. But however, complicated a single proposition may be, no brother has a right to insist upon its division. His remedy is to move that it be divided, if it is capable of division, or, if not, to move to strike out the objectionable parts. A motion to strike out a name in a resolution brings the lodge to a vote on that name just as well as would a division of the question, if it were allowed to go to that extent, which it is not. If a series of resolutions is proposed as a substitute for another series, such a motion is incapable of division; but a motion can be made to strike out any of the resolutions before the vote is taken on the substitution. After they have been substituted it is too late to strike out any of them. When a committee reports a number of amendments to a resolution referred to it, one vote may be taken on adopting, or agreeing to, all the amendments provided no one objects. But if a single brother requests separate votes on one or more of the amendments, they must be considered separately. The others may all be voted on together.

Consideration by Paragraph or Seriatim. Where an elaborate proposition is submitted, like a series of resolutions on one subject, or a set of bylaws, the parts being intimately connected, it should not be divided. The division would add greatly to the difficulty of perfecting the different paragraphs or bylaws by amendments. If the paragraphs are adopted separately, and amendments to succeeding paragraphs make it necessary to amend a preceding one, it can be done only by first reconsidering the vote on the preceding paragraph. In the case of bylaws, the trouble is increased, because each bylaw goes into effect as soon as adopted, and its amendment is controlled by any bylaw or rule that may have been adopted on the subject. When the paragraphs are voted on separately no vote should be taken on the whole. But in all such cases the proper course is to consider the proposition by paragraph, or section, or resolution, or, as it is often called, *seriatim*. The W. M. should always adopt this course when the question consists of several paragraphs or resolutions, unless he thinks the lodge wishes to act on them immediately as a whole, when he asks if they shall be taken up by paragraph, and the matter is settled informally. Should the W. M. neglect to take up the proposition by paragraph, anyone may move that the proposition be considered by paragraph, or seriatim.

The method of procedure in acting upon a complicated report, as, a set of bylaws, or a series of resolutions that cannot well be divided, is as follows, the word "paragraph" being used to designate the natural subdivisions, whether they are paragraphs, sections, articles, or resolutions. The brother submitting the report, having obtained the floor says that such and such committee submits the following report; or, that the committee recommends the adoption of the following resolutions. In either case he reads the report, or resolutions, and moves their adoption. Should he neglect to move their adoption, the W. M. should call for such a motion, or he may assume the motion and state the question accordingly. The W. M., or the secretary, or the brother who reported it (whoever the W. M. decides is for the best interest of the lodge) then reads the first paragraph, which is explained by the reporting brother, after which the W. M. asks, "Are there any amendments to this paragraph?" The paragraph is then open to debate and amendment. When no further amendments are proposed to this paragraph, the W. M. says, "There being no further amendments to this paragraph the next will be read." In a similar manner each paragraph in succession is read, explained if necessary, debated, and amended, the paragraphs being amended but not adopted. After all the paragraphs have been amended, the W. M. says the entire by-law, or paper, or resolution is open to amendment, when additional paragraphs may be inserted, and any paragraph may be further amended. When the paper is satisfactorily amended, the preamble, if any, is treated the same way, and then a single vote is taken on the adoption of the entire paper, report, or series of resolutions. If the previous question is ordered on a resolution, or series of resolutions, or on a set of bylaws, before the preamble has been considered it does not apply to the preamble, unless expressly so stated, because the preamble cannot be considered until after debate has ceased on the resolutions or bylaws. It is not necessary to amend the numbers of the sections, paragraphs, etc., as it is the duty of the secretary to make all such corrections where changes are rendered necessary by amendments.

25. Division of the Lodge, and other Motions relating to Voting.

A Division of the Lodge may be called for, without obtaining the floor, at any time after the question has been put, even after the vote has been announced and another has the floor, provided the vote was taken by voice or by show of hands, and it is called for before another motion has been made. This call, or motion, is made by saying, "I call for a division," or "I doubt the vote," or simply by calling out, "Division." It does not require a second, and cannot be debated, or amended, or have any other subsidiary motion applied to it. As soon as a division is called for, the W. M. proceeds again to take the vote, this time by having the affirmative rise, and then when they are seated having the negative rise. While any brother has the right to request a rising vote, or a division, where there is any question as to the vote being a true expression of the will of the lodge, the W. M. should not permit this privilege to be abused to the annoyance of the lodge, by brothers constantly demanding a division where there is a full vote and no question as to which side is in the majority. It requires a majority vote to order the vote to be counted, or to be taken by yeas and nays (roll call) or by ballot. These motions are incidental to the question that is pending or has just been pending and cannot be debated. When different methods are suggested, they are usually treated not as amendments, but like filling blanks, the vote being taken first on the one taking the most time. In practice the method of taking a vote is generally agreed upon without the formality of a vote.

When the vote is taken by ballot during a meeting of the lodge, as soon as the W. M. thinks all have voted, he inquires if all have voted, and if there is no response, he declares the ballot closed, and orders the ballot displayed (counted).

26. Motions relating to Nominations.

If no method of making nominations is designated by the lodge or Grand Lodge constitution, bylaws or rules, and the lodge has adopted no order on the subject, anyone can make a motion prescribing the method of nomination for an office to be filled. If the election is pending, this motion is incidental to it; if the election is not pending, it is an incidental main motion. It is undebatable and when it is an incidental motion it can have no subsidiary motion applied to it except to amend. It yields to privileged motions. The motion may provide for nominations being made by the W. M.; or from the floor, or open nominations as it is also called; or for a nominating committee to be appointed. [See Nominations and Elections, **64**.]

Closing and Reopening Nominations. Before proceeding to an election, if nominations have been made from the floor or by a committee, the W. M. should inquire if there are any further nominations. If there is no response, he declares the nominations closed. In very large bodies it is customary to make a motion to close nominations, but until a reasonable time has been given, this motion is not in order. It is a main motion, incidental to the nominations and elections, cannot be debated, can be amended as to the time, but can have no other subsidiary motion applied to it. It yields to privileged motions, and requires a two-thirds vote as it deprives brothers of one of their rights.

If for any reason it is desired to reopen nominations it may be done by a majority vote. This motion is undebatable. It can be amended as to the time, but no other subsidiary motion can be applied to it. It yields to privileged motions.

27. Requests Growing out of the Business of the Lodge.

During the meetings of a lodge there are occasions when members wish to obtain information, or to do or to have done things that necessitate their making a request. Among these are the following, which will be treated separately:

(a) Parliamentary Inquiry;
(b) Request for Information;
(c) Leave to Withdraw a Motion;
(d) Reading Papers;
(e) To be Excused from a Duty;
(f) For any other Privilege.

(a) Parliamentary Inquiry. A parliamentary inquiry, if it relates to a question that requires immediate attention, may be made while

another has the floor, or may even interrupt a speech. It should not, however, be permitted to interrupt a speaker any more than is necessary to do justice to the inquirer. It yields to privileged motions, if they were in order when the inquiry was made, and it cannot be debated, amended, or have any other subsidiary motion applied to it. The inquirer does not obtain the floor, but rises and says, "W. M., I rise to a parliamentary inquiry." The W. M. asks him to state his inquiry, and if he deems it pertinent, he answers it. Or, if the inquiry is made when another has the floor, and there is no necessity for answering it until the speech is finished, the W. M. may defer his answer until the speaker has closed his remarks. While it is not the duty of the W. M. to answer questions of parliamentary law in general, it is his duty when requested by a brother, to answer any questions on parliamentary law pertinent to the pending business that may be necessary to enable the brother to make a suitable motion or to raise a point of order. The W. M. is supposed to be familiar with parliamentary law, while many of the brothers are not. A brother wishing to raise a point of order and yet in doubt, should rise to a parliamentary inquiry and ask for information. Or, for instance, he may wish to have the lodge act immediately on a subject that is in the hands of a committee, and he does not know how to accomplish it; — his recourse is a parliamentary inquiry.

(b) *Request for Information.* A request for information relating to the pending business is treated just as a parliamentary inquiry, and has the same privileges. The inquirer rises and says, "W. M., I rise for information," or, "I rise to a point of information," whereupon the W. M. directs him to state the point upon which he desires information, and the procedure continues as in case of a parliamentary inquiry. If the information is desired of the speaker, instead of the W. M., the inquirer upon rising says, "W. M., I should like to ask the brother a question." The W. M. inquires if the speaker is willing to be interrupted, and if he consents, he directs the inquirer to proceed. The inquirer then asks the question through the W. M., thus, "W. M., I should like to ask the brother," etc. The reply is made in the same way, as it is not in order for brothers to address one another in the lodge during a speech (question and answer periods excepted). While each speaker addresses the W. M., the W. M. remains silent during the conversation. If the speaker consents to the interruption the time consumed is taken out of his time.

(c) Leave to Withdraw or Modify a Motion. A request for leave to withdraw a motion, or a motion to grant such leave, may be made at any time before voting on the question has commenced, even though the motion has been amended. It requires no second. It may be made while incidental or subsidiary motions are pending, and these motions cease to be before the lodge when the question to which they are incidental, or subsidiary is withdrawn. It yields to privileged motions, and cannot be amended or have any other subsidiary motion applied to it. It is undebatable. When it is too late to renew it, the motion to reconsider cannot be withdrawn without unanimous consent. When a motion is withdrawn, the effect is the same as if it had never been made. Until a motion is stated by the W. M., the mover may withdraw or modify it without asking consent of anyone. If he modifies it the seconder may withdraw his second. When the mover requests permission to modify or withdraw his motion, the W. M. asks if there is any objection, and if there is none, he announces that the motion is withdrawn or modified in such and such a way, as the case may be. If anyone objects the W. M. puts the question on granting the request, or a motion may be made to grant it. In case the mover of a main motion wishes to accept an amendment that has been offered, without obtaining the floor, he says, "W. M., I accept the amendment." If no objection is made the W. M. announces the question as amended. If anyone objects, the W. M. states the question on the amendment, as it can be accepted only by general consent. A request for leave to do anything is treated the same as a motion to grant the leave except that the request must be made by the maker of the motion it is proposed to modify, while the motion to grant the leave is made by someone else and therefore requires no second as it is favored by the one making the request.

(d) Reading Papers. If any brother objects, a brother has no right to read, or have the secretary read, from any paper or book, as a part of his speech, without the permission of the lodge. The request or the motion to grant such permission yields to privileged motions. It cannot be debated, or amended, or have any other subsidiary motion applied to it. It is customary, however, to allow brothers to read

printed extracts as parts of their speeches, as long as they do not abuse the privilege.

Where papers are laid before the lodge, every brother has a right to have them read once, or if there is debate or amendment, he has the right to have them read again, before he can be compelled to vote on them. Whenever a brother asks for the reading of any such paper evidently for information, and not for delay, the W. M. should direct it to be read, if no one objects. But a brother has not the right to have anything read (excepting as stated above) without permission of the lodge. If a brother was absent from the hall when the paper under consideration was read, even though absent on duty, he cannot insist on its being again read, as the convenience of the lodge is of more importance than that of a single brother.

(e) To be Excused from a Duty. If a brother is elected or appointed to office, or appointed on a committee, or has any other duty placed on him, and he is unable or unwilling to perform the duty, if present he should decline it immediately, and if absent he should, upon learning of the fact, at once notify the secretary or W.M. orally or in writing that he cannot accept the duty. In most organizations members cannot be compelled to accept office or perform any duties not required by the bylaws, and therefore they have the right to decline office. But if a brother does not immediately decline, by his silence he accepts the office, and is under obligation to perform the duty until there has been a reasonable opportunity for his resignation (by proper means) to be accepted. The secretary, for instance, cannot relieve himself from the responsibility of his office by resigning. His responsibility as secretary does not cease until his resignation is accepted, or, at least, until there has been a reasonable time for its acceptance. It is seldom good policy to decline to accept a resignation. As a brother has no right to continue to hold an office the duties of which he cannot or will not perform, so a lodge has no right to force an office on an unwilling brother. When a brother declines an office, no motion is necessary, unless the bylaws of the lodge make the performance of such duties obligatory upon members. If the brother is present at the election, the vacancy is filled as if no one had been elected. A new election may be in order. If the brother was not present at the election, when the W. M. announces his refusal to take

the office, as it is a question of privilege relating to the organization of the lodge, the election to fill the vacancy may take place at once unless notice is required, or other provision for filling vacancies is provided by the bylaws or Grand Lodge. In the case of a resignation, the W. M. may at once state the question on accepting it, or a motion to that effect may be made. In either case it is debatable and may have any subsidiary motion applied to it. It yields to privileged and incidental motions.

(f) *Request for Any Other Privilege.* When any request is to be made the brother rises and addresses the W. M., and as soon as he catches the eye of the W. M., states at once why he rises. He should rise as soon as a brother yields the floor, and, though the floor is assigned to another, he still makes his request. He should never interrupt a brother while speaking unless he is sure that the urgency of the case justifies it. As a rule, all such questions are settled by general consent, or informally, but, if objection is made, a vote is taken. An explanation may be requested or given, but there is no debate. As these requests arise, they should be treated so as to interrupt the proceedings as little as is consistent with the demands of justice.

Art. V

Subsidiary Motions

28. To Lay on the Table
29. The Previous Question
30. Limit or Extend Limits of Debate
31. To Postpone to a Certain Time
32. To Commit or Refer
33. To Amend
34. To Postpone Indefinitely

28. To Lay on the Table.

This motion takes precedence of all other subsidiary [12] motions and of such incidental [13] questions as are pending at the time it is made. It yields to privileged [14] motions and such motions as are incidental to itself. It is undebatable and cannot have any subsidiary motion applied to it. It may be applied to any main [11] motion; to any question of privilege or order of the day, after it is before the lodge for consideration; to an appeal that does not adhere to the main question, so that the action on the latter would not be affected by the reversal of the W. M.'s decision; or to the motion to reconsider when immediately pending, in which case the question to be reconsidered goes to the table also. No motion that has another motion adhering to it can be laid on the table by itself; if laid on the table it carries with it everything that adheres to it. When a motion is taken from the table [35] everything is in the same condition, as far as practicable, as when the motion was laid on the table, except that if not taken up until the next meeting the effect of the previous question is exhausted. If debate has been closed by ordering the previous question, or otherwise, up to the moment of taking the last vote under the order, the questions still before the lodge may be laid on the table. Thus, if, while a resolution, an amendment, and a motion to commit are pending, the previous question is ordered on the series of questions, and the vote has been taken and lost on the motion to commit, it is in order to lay on the table the resolution, which carries with it the adhering amendment.

This motion cannot be applied to anything except a question pending, therefore it is not in order to lay on the table a class of questions, as the orders of the day, or unfinished business, or reports of committees, because they are not pending questions, as only one main motion can be pending at a time.

To accomplish the desired object, which is evidently to reach a special subject or class of business, the proper course is for the W.M. to suspend the rules (order of business) and take up the desired question or class of business. Sometimes when it is desired to pass over the next order or class of business, that business is "passed," as it is called. In such case, as soon as the business for which it was "passed" is disposed of, it is then taken up. The business to come before the lodge may be considered in any order the W.M. desires.

If a motion to lay on the table has been made and lost, or if a question laid on the table has been taken from the table, it shows that the lodge wishes to consider the question now, and therefore a motion made the same day to lay that question on the table is out of order until there has been material progress in business or debate, or unless an unforeseen urgent matter requires immediate attention. The lodge cannot be required to vote again the same day on laying the question on the table unless there is such a change in the state of affairs as to make it a new question. A vote on laying on the table cannot be reconsidered, because, if lost the motion may be renewed as soon as there has been material progress in debate or business, or even before if anything unforeseen occurs of such an urgent nature as to require immediate attention; and if adopted the question may be taken from the table as soon as the interrupting business has been disposed of and while no question is pending, and business of this class, or new or unfinished business, is in order.

The *Form* of this motion is, "I move to lay the question on the table," or, "That the question be laid on the table," or, "That the question lie on the table." If it is qualified, thus, "To lay the question on the table until 8 P.M.," the W. M. should state it properly as a motion to postpone until 8 P.M., which is a debatable question, and not the motion to lay on the table.

The *Object* of this motion is to enable the lodge, in order to attend to more urgent business, to lay aside the pending question in such a way that its consideration may be resumed as easily as if it were a new question, and in preference to new questions competing with it for consideration. It is to the interest of the lodge that this object should be attained instantly by a majority vote, and therefore this motion must either apply to, or take precedence of, every debatable motion whatever its rank. It is undebatable, and requires only a majority vote, notwithstanding the fact that if not taken from the table the question is suppressed. These are dangerous privileges which are given to no other motion whose adoption would result in final action on a main motion. There is a great temptation to make an improper use of them, and lay questions on the table for the purpose of instantly suppressing them by a majority vote, instead of using the previous question, the legitimate motion to bring the lodge to an immediate vote. The fundamental principles of parliamentary law require a two-thirds vote for every motion that suppresses a main question for the meeting without free debate. The motion to lay on the table being undebatable, and requiring only a majority vote, and having the highest rank of all subsidiary motions, is in direct conflict with these principles, if used to suppress a question. If habitually used in this way, it should, like the other motions to suppress without debate, require a two-thirds vote.

The minority has no remedy for the unfair use of this motion, but the harm can be slightly diminished as follows: The person who introduces a resolution is sometimes cut off from speaking by the motion to lay the question on the table being made as soon as the W. M. states the question, or even before. In such cases the introducer of the resolution should always claim the floor, to which he is entitled, and make his speech. Persons are commonly in such a hurry to make this motion that they neglect to address the W. M. and thus obtain the floor. In such case one of the minority should address the W. M. quickly, and if not given the floor, make the point of order that he is the first one to address the W. M., and that the other brother, not having the floor, was not entitled to make a motion [3].

As motions laid on the table are merely temporarily laid aside, the majority should remember that the minority may all stay to the moment of final adjournment and then be in the majority, and take up and pass the resolutions laid on the table. They may also take the question from the table at the next meeting. The safer and fairer method is to object to the consideration of the question if it is so objectionable that it is not desired to allow even its introducer to speak on it; or, if there has been debate so it cannot be objected to, then to move the previous question, which, if adopted, immediately brings the lodge to a vote. These are legitimate motions for getting at the sense of the brothers at once as to whether they wish the subject discussed, and, as they require a two-thirds vote, no one has a right to object to their being adopted.

The *Effect* of the adoption of this motion is to place on the table, that is, in charge of the secretary, the pending question and everything adhering to it; so, if an amendment is pending to a motion to refer a resolution to a committee, and the question is laid on the table, all these questions go together to the table, and when taken from the table they all come up together. An amendment proposed to anything already adopted is a main motion, and therefore when laid on the table, does not carry with it the thing proposed to be amended. A question of privilege may be laid on the table without carrying with it the question it interrupted. The reasons for any one of these rules apply with nearly equal force to the others. While a question is on the table no motion on the same subject is in order that would in any way affect the question that is on the table; it is necessary first to take the question from the table and move the new one as a substitute, or to make such other motion as is adapted to the case.

29. The Previous Question

The Previous Question takes precedence of all subsidiary [12] motions except to lay on the table and yields to privileged [14] and incidental [13] motions, and to the motion to lay on the table. It is undebatable, and cannot be amended or have any other subsidiary motion applied to it. The effect of an amendment may be obtained by calling for, or moving, the previous question on a different set of the pending questions (which must be consecutive and include the immediately pending question), in which case the vote is taken first on the motion which orders the previous question on the largest number of questions. It may be applied to any debatable or amendable motion or motions, and if unqualified it applies only to the immediately pending motion. It may be qualified so as to apply to a series of pending questions, or to a consecutive part of a series beginning with the immediately pending question. It requires a two-thirds vote for its adoption. After the previous question has been ordered, up to the time of taking the last vote under it, the questions that have not been voted on may be laid on the table, but can have no other subsidiary motions applied to them. An appeal made after the previous question has been demanded or ordered and before its exhaustion, is undebatable. The previous question, before any vote has been taken under it, may be reconsidered, but not after its partial execution. As no one would vote to reconsider the vote ordering the previous question who was not opposed to the previous question, it follows that if the motion to reconsider prevails, it will be impossible to secure a two-thirds vote for the previous question, and, therefore, if it is voted to reconsider the previous question it is considered as rejecting that question and placing the business as it was before the previous question was moved. If a vote taken under the previous question is reconsidered before the previous question is exhausted, there can be no debate or amendment of the proposition; but if the reconsideration is after the previous question is exhausted, then the motion to reconsider, as well as the question to be reconsidered, is divested of the previous question and is debatable. If lost, the previous question may be renewed after sufficient progress in debate to make it a new question.

The *Form* of this motion is, "I move [or demand, or call for] the previous question on [here specify the motions on which it is desired to be ordered]." As it cannot be debated or amended, it must be voted on immediately. The form of putting the question is, "The previous question is moved [or demanded, or called for] on [specify the motions on which the previous question is demanded].

As many as are in favor of ordering the previous question on [repeat the motions] will rise." When they are seated, he continues, "Those opposed will rise. There being two-thirds in favor of the motion, the affirmative has it and the previous question is ordered on [repeat the motions upon which it is ordered]. The question is [or recurs] on [state the immediately pending question]. As many as are in favor," etc. If the previous question is ordered the W. M. immediately proceeds to put to vote the questions on which it was ordered until all the votes are taken, or there is an affirmative vote on postponing definitely or indefinitely, or committing, either of which exhausts the previous question. If there can be the slightest doubt as to the vote the W. M. should take it again immediately, counting each side. If less than two-thirds vote in the affirmative, the W. M. announces the vote thus: "There not being two-thirds in favor of the motion, the negative has it and the motion is lost. The question is on," etc., the W. M. stating the question on the immediately pending question, which is again open to debate and amendment, the same as if the previous question had not been demanded.

The question may be put in a form similar to this: "The previous question has been moved on the motion to commit and its amendment. As many as are in favor of now putting the question on the motion to commit and its amendment will rise; those opposed will rise. There being two-thirds in favor of the motion, the debate is closed on the motion to commit and its amendment, and the question is on the amendment," etc. While this form is allowable, yet it is better to conform to the regular parliamentary form as given above.

The *Object* of the previous question is to bring the lodge at once to a vote on the immediately pending question and on such other pending questions as may be specified in the demand. It is the proper motion to use for this purpose, whether the object is to adopt or to kill the proposition on which it is ordered, without further debate or motions to amend.

The *Effect* of ordering the previous question is to close debate immediately, to prevent the moving of amendments or any other subsidiary motions except to lay on the table, and to bring the lodge at once to a vote on the immediately pending question, and such other pending questions as were specified in the demand, or motion. If the previous question is ordered on more than one question, then its effect extends to those questions and is not exhausted until they are voted on, or they are disposed of as shown below under exhaustion of the previous question. If the previous question is voted down, the discussion continues as if this motion had not been made. The effect of the previous question does not extend beyond the meeting in which it was adopted. Should any of the questions upon which it was ordered come before the lodge at a future meeting they are divested of the previous question and are open to debate and amendment.

The previous question is *Exhausted* during the meeting as follows:

(1) When the previous question is unqualified, its effect terminates as soon as the vote is taken on the immediately pending question.

(2) If the previous question is ordered on more than one of the pending questions its effect is not exhausted until all of the questions upon which it has been ordered have been voted on, or else the effect of those that have been voted on has been to commit the main question, or to postpone it definitely or indefinitely.

If, before the exhaustion of the previous question, the questions on which it has been ordered that have not been voted on are laid on the table, the previous question is not exhausted thereby, so that when they are taken from the table during the same meeting, they are still under the previous question and cannot be debated, amended, or have any other subsidiary motion applied to them.

NOTE ON THE PREVIOUS QUESTION. – Much of the confusion heretofore existing in regard to the Previous Question has arisen from the great changes which this motion has undergone. As originally designed, the previous question was not intended to suppress debate, but to suppress the main question, and therefore, it is commonly moved by the enemies of the measure, who then vote in the negative. It was first used in 1604, and was intended to be applied only to delicate questions; it was put in this form, "Shall the main question be put?" and being voted down, the main question was dismissed for that meeting. Its form was afterwards changed to this, which is used at present, "Shall the main question be now put?" and if voted down the question was dismissed, at first only until after the ensuing debate was over, but now, for that day. The motion for the previous question could be debated; when once put to vote, whether decided affirmatively or negatively, it prevented any discussion of the main question, for, if decided affirmatively, the main question was immediately put, and if decided negatively (that is, that the main question be not now put), it was dismissed for the day.

30. Limit or Extend Limits of Debate.

Motions, or orders, to limit or extend the limits of debate, like the previous question, take precedence of all debatable motions, may be applied to any debatable motion or series of motions, and, if not specified to the contrary, apply only to the immediately pending question. If it is voted to limit the debate, the order applies to all incidental and subsidiary motions and the motion to reconsider, subsequently made, as long as the order is in force. But an order extending the limits of debate does not apply to any motions except the immediately pending one and such others as are specified. They are undebatable, and require a two-thirds vote for their adoption. These motions may be amended, but can have no other subsidiary motion applied to them. They yield to privileged [14] and incidental [13] motions, and to the motions to lay on the table and for the previous question. They may be made only when the immediately pending question is debatable. When one of them is pending, another one that does not conflict with it may be moved as an amendment. After one of these motions has been adopted it is in order to move another one of them, provided it does not conflict with the one in force. This motion to limit or extend the limits of debate may be reconsidered even though the order has been partially executed, and if lost it may be renewed after there has been sufficient progress in debate to make it a new question.

After an order is adopted closing debate at a certain hour, or limiting it to a certain time, the motions to postpone and to commit cannot be moved until the vote adopting the order has been reconsidered; but the pending question may be laid on the table, and if it is not taken from the table until after the hour appointed for closing the debate and taking the vote, no debate or motion to amend is allowed, as the W. M. should immediately put the question. After the adoption of an order limiting the number or length of the speeches, or extending these limits, it is in order to move any of the other subsidiary [12] motions on the pending question.

An order modifying the limits of debate on a question is in force only during the meeting in which it was adopted. If the question in any way goes over to the next meeting it is divested of this order and is open to debate according to the regular rules.

The various *Forms* of this motion are as follows:

(1) To fix the time for closing debate and putting the question, the form is similar to this: "I move that debate close and the question be put on the resolution at 8 P.M."

(2) To limit the length of the debate, the motion may be made thus: "I move that debate on the pending amendment be limited to twenty minutes."

(3) To reduce or increase the number and length of speeches, the motion should be made in a form similar to one of these: "I move that debate on the pending resolution and its amendments be limited to one speech of five minutes from each brother;" "I move that Br. A's time be extended ten minutes;" "I move that Bros. A and B (the leaders on the two sides) be allowed twenty minutes each, to be divided between their two speeches at their pleasure, and that other brothers be limited to one speech of two minutes each, and that the question be put at 9 P.M."

31. To Postpone to a Certain Time

To postpone to a certain time takes precedence of the motions to commit, to amend, and to postpone indefinitely, and yields to all privileged [14] and incidental [13] motions, and to the motions to lay on the table, for the previous question, and to limit or to extend the limits of debate. It allows for a limited debate which must not go into the merits of the main question any more than is necessary to enable the lodge to determine the propriety of the postponement. It may be amended as to the time, and also by making the postponed question a special order. The previous question and the motions limiting or extending the limits of debate may be applied to it. It cannot be laid on the table alone, but when it is pending the main question may be laid on the table which carries with it the motion to postpone. It cannot be committed or postponed indefinitely. It may be reconsidered. When it makes a question a special order it requires a two-thirds vote.

The time to which a question is postponed must fall within the meeting or the next meeting, and, if it is desired to postpone it to a different time, which must not be beyond the next regular meeting. Neither the motion to postpone indefinitely nor an amendment to it, is in order when it has the effect of an indefinite postponement; that is, to defeat the measure, as, for instance, to postpone until next meeting a motion to accept an invitation to a banquet tonight. If the motion to postpone indefinitely is in order at the time, the W. M. may treat it as such at his discretion, but it cannot be recognized as a motion to postpone indefinitely. It is not in order to postpone a class of business, as reports of committees; as each report is announced or called for, it may be postponed, or the rules may be suspended by a two-thirds vote and the desired question be taken up. A matter that is required by the bylaws to be attended to at a specified time or meeting as the election of officers cannot, in advance, be postponed to another time or meeting. This is sometimes advisable as in case of an annual meeting for the election of officers occurring on a very stormy night so that a bare quorum is present. [If elections are required by Grand Lodge law to be held on a certain meeting, then the elections cannot be postponed.] After an order of the day or a question of privilege is before the lodge for action, its further consideration may be postponed, or any other subsidiary motion may be applied to it. When a question has been postponed to a certain time, it becomes an order of the day for that time and cannot be taken up before that time except by a reconsideration, or by suspending the rules for that purpose, which requires a two-thirds vote. [See Orders of the Day, **20**, for the treatment of questions that have been postponed definitely.]

The *Form* of this motion depends upon the object sought.

(1) If the object is simply to postpone the question to the next meeting, when it will have precedence of new business, the form of the motion is "to postpone the question [or, that the question be postponed] to the next meeting." It then becomes a general order for that meeting.

(2) If the object is to specify an hour when the question will be taken up as soon as the question then pending, if there is any, is disposed of, the form is similar to this: "I move that the question be postponed to 8 P.M."

(3) If it is desired to postpone the question until after a certain event, when it shall immediately come up, the form is, "To postpone the question until after the address on Ritual."

(4) If the object is to insure it's not being crowded out by other matters there should be added to the motion to postpone as given in

the first two cases above, the words, "and be made a special order." Or the motion may be made thus: "I move that the question be postponed and made a special order for the next meeting [or, for 8 P.M. tomorrow]." The motion in this form requires a two-thirds vote, as it suspends the rules that may interfere with its consideration at the time specified as explained under Orders of the Day [20].

(5) If it is desired to postpone a question to a certain meeting and devote the entire time, if necessary, to its consideration, as in case of revising bylaws, after providing for the meeting the motion should be made in this form: "I move that the question be postponed and made the special order for the first meeting in May." Or a question may be postponed and made the special order for the next regular meeting.

The *Effect* of postponing a question is to make it an order of the day for the time to which it was postponed, and if it is not then disposed of, it becomes unfinished business. Postponing a question to a certain hour does not make it a special order unless so specified in the motion. The motion to postpone definitely may be amended by a majority vote so as to make the amended motion one to make the question a special order. If this is done the amended motion will require a two-thirds vote. [Orders of the Day, **20**, should be read in connection with this section.]

32. To Commit or Refer.

(All the rules in regard to this motion, except where stated to the contrary, apply equally to the motions to Go into Committee of the Whole, to Consider Informally, and to Recommit as it is called when a question is committed a second time.) This motion takes precedence of the motions to amend and to postpone indefinitely, and yields to all the other subsidiary [12] motions and to all privileged [14] and incidental [13] motions. It cannot be applied to any subsidiary motion, nor can it be laid on the table or postponed except in connection with the main question. The previous question, and motions to limit or extend the limits of debate, and to amend, may be applied, to it without affecting the main question. It is debatable but only as to the propriety of committing the main question. If the motion to postpone indefinitely is pending when a question is referred to a committee, it is lost, and is not referred to the committee. Pending amendments go with the main motion to the committee. The motion to commit may be reconsidered, but after the committee has begun the consideration of the question referred to it, it is too late to move to reconsider the vote to commit. The committee may, however, then be discharged as shown below.

The motion to commit (that is, to refer to a committee) may vary in form all the way from the simple form of, "That the question be referred to a committee," to the complete form of referring to question "to a committee of five to be appointed by the W. M., with instructions to report resolutions properly covering the case, at the next regular business meeting." If the motion is made in the complete form the details may be changed by amendments, though they are usually treated not as ordinary amendments, but as in filling blanks [33:14].

If the motion is made in the simple form of merely referring the pending question to a committee there are three courses that may be pursued in completing the details, the one to be chosen depending upon the circumstances of the case. (1) The simple, or skeleton, motion may be completed by moving amendments, or making suggestions, for adding the required details as stated below. (2) The W. M. on his own initiative may call for suggestions to complete the motion, first inquiring as to what committee the question shall be referred, and continuing in the order shown hereafter. (3) The motion in its simplest form may be put to vote at once by its opponents' ordering the previous question, and where the motion to commit is almost certain to be lost this is sometimes done to save the time that would be uselessly spent in completing the details. If it should happen that the motion to commit is adopted, which is improbable, then the details are completed before any new business, except privileged matters, can be taken up. These details are taken up in the order given below, the W. M. calling for the several items much as if he were completing the motion before it was voted on.

In completing a motion simply to refer to a committee, the first question the W. M. asks is, "To what committee shall the question be referred?" If different ones are suggested, the suggestions are not treated as amendments of those previously offered, but are voted on in the following order until one receives a majority vote: Committee of the whole; as if in committee of the whole; consider informally; standing committee, in the order in which they are proposed; special (select) committee (largest number voted on first). If the question has already been before a standing or special committee the motion becomes the motion to recommit, and the committees would be voted on in the above order except the old committee would precede other standing and select committees. In suggesting or moving that the committee be a special one, the word "special" is not generally used, the motion being made to refer the question to a committee of five, or any other number, which makes it a special committee; that is, not a standing committee. If any committee except a special one is decided upon, the W. M. should then put the question on referring the question to that committee. Instructions by the W.M. may be given after the vote has been taken on committing the question.

The W.M. shall appoint all members of committees. The W.M. may ask for volunteers to sit on the committee, but the final decision as to the membership of all committees rests with him. When the committee is named, the completed motion to commit is put to vote. Instructions as heretofore stated may be added before the vote is taken on the motion to commit, or they may be given afterwards. If the motion to commit is adopted, no new business, except privileged matters, can intervene until the appointment of the committee by the Worshipful Master.

The *Forms* of this motion are as follows: "To refer the question to a committee;" "To recommit the resolution;" "That the subject be referred to a committee of three to be appointed by the W. M., and that it report by resolution at the next meeting;" "That it be referred to a committee with power;" etc., specifying the subject [55]; "That the resolution be considered as if in committee of the whole" [56]; "That the resolution be considered informally" [57].

The *Object* of the motion to refer to a standing or special committee is usually to enable a question to be more carefully investigated and put into better shape for the lodge to consider, than can be done in the lodge itself. Where a lodge is large and has a very large amount of business it is safer to have some main questions go to a committee before final action on it is taken. A special committee to investigate and report upon a subject should consist of representative members on both sides of the question, so that both parties in the lodge may have confidence in the report, or reports in case there is disagreement, and a minority report is submitted. It is not at all necessary to appoint on the committee the brother who makes the motion to refer, but it is usual, and the courteous thing to do, when he is specially interested or informed on the subject.

Sometimes a question is referred to a committee with full power to act in the case. When the duty assigned it has been performed, it should report what it has done, and when this report has been made the committee ceases to exist. An example would be a committee formed to determine a qualified photographer for an upcoming installation of officers. If the committee is charged with evaluating and contracting the photographer, their duty is fulfilled upon reporting to the lodge that they have secured the services of a photographer for the event. When the lodge has decided a question and appoints a committee to take certain action (such as a committee of arrangements for holding a public meeting), then the committee should be small, and all should be favorable to the action to be taken. If anyone is appointed on such a committee who is not in sympathy with the proposed action, he should say so and ask to be excused. Sometimes such a committee is given power to add to its number.

The object of going into committee of the whole, or considering a question as if in committee of the whole, or informally, is to enable the lodge to discuss a question with perfect freedom, there being no limit to the number of speeches.

If any form of the motion to commit is made with reference to a question not pending, it becomes a main motion. Thus, a motion to go into committee of the whole on a question not pending, or to appoint a committee upon a subject not pending, or to appoint a committee to take certain action, is a main motion.

To Discharge a Committee. When a committee has made its final report and it has been received by the lodge, the committee ceases to exist without any additional motion being made to that effect. When the committee is discharged, its chairman returns to the Secretary any and all papers that have been entrusted to him. It requires a motion to bring the matter referred before the lodge, and this motion may, however, be combined with the motion to discharge, thus: "I move that the committee to whom was referred the resolution on dues be discharged, and that the resolution be now taken up for consideration [or, be considered at some other specified time]."

33. To Amend

To Amend takes precedence of the motion to postpone indefinitely and yields to all other subsidiary [12] motions and to all privileged [14] and incidental [13] motions, except the motion to divide the question. It can be applied to all motions except those in the List of Motions that Cannot be Amended [33:12]. It can be amended itself, but this "amendment of an amendment" (an amendment of the second degree) cannot be amended. The previous question and motions to limit or extend the limits of debate may be applied to an amendment, or to only an amendment of an amendment, and in such case, they do not affect the main question, unless so specified. An amendment is debatable in all cases except where the motion to be amended is undebatable. An amendment of a pending question requires only a majority vote for its adoption, even though the question to be amended requires a two-thirds vote. An amendment of a constitution or bylaws, or rules of order, or order of business, previously adopted, requires a two-thirds vote; but an amendment of that amendment requires only a majority vote. When a motion or resolution is under consideration only one amendment of the first degree is permitted at a time, and one amendment of that amendment — that is, an amendment of the second degree is allowed also. An amendment of the third degree would be too complicated and is not in order. Instead of making it, a brother may say that if the amendment of the amendment is voted down, he will offer such and such an amendment of the amendment. While there can be only one amendment of each degree pending at the same time, any number of them may be offered in succession. An amendment must be germane to the subject to be amended — that is, it must relate to it, as shown further on. So, an amendment to an amendment must be germane to the latter.

Form. An amendment may be in any of the following forms: (a) to *insert* or *add* (that is, place at the end); (b) to *strike out*; (c) to *strike out* and *insert*, or to *substitute*, as it is called, when an entire paragraph or resolution is struck out and another is inserted. The third form is a combination of the other two and cannot be divided, though, as shown hereafter, for the purposes of amendment the two motions are treated separately, the words to be struck out being first amended and then the words to be inserted. No amendment is in order which will convert one of these forms into another.

The motion to amend is made in a form similar to this: "I move to amend the resolution by inserting the word 'very' before the word 'good;'" or, it may be reduced to a form as simple as this: "I move to insert 'very' before 'good.'" The motion to insert should always specify the word before or after which the insertion is to be made. The motion to strike out should also locate the word, provided it occurs more than once. When the W. M. states the question on the amendment, he should repeat the motion in detail so that all may understand what modification is proposed. Unless the effect of the amendment is very evident, he should, in putting the question, clearly show the effect of its adoption, even though it requires the reading of the entire resolution, and then the words to be inserted, or struck out, or struck out and inserted, and finally the resolution as it will stand if the amendment is adopted. He then says, "As many as are in favor of the amendment [or, of striking out, etc., or of inserting, etc.] say *aye*; those opposed, say *no*. The ayes have it, the amendment is adopted, and the question is on the resolution as amended, which is, '*Resolved*, That,'" etc., reading the resolution as amended. If the vote is taken by show of hands or by rising, the question is put and the vote announced thus: "As many as are in favor of the amendment will rise [or, will raise the right hand]; those opposed will rise [or, will signify it in the same way]. The affirmative has it and the amendment is adopted. The question is on the resolution," etc. The instant the amendment is voted on, whether it is adopted or lost, the W. M. should announce the result of the vote and state the question that is then before the lodge.

To *Insert* or *Add Words*. When a motion to insert [or add] certain words is made, the words to be inserted should be perfected by amendments proposed by their friends before the vote is taken on inserting or adding them. After words have been inserted or added, they cannot be changed or struck out except by a motion to strike out the paragraph, or such a portion of it as shall make the question an entirely different one from that of inserting the particular words; or by combining such a motion to strike out the paragraph or a portion of it with the motion to insert other words. The principle involved is that when the lodge has voted that certain words shall form a part of a resolution; it is not in order to make another motion that involves exactly the same question as the one it has decided. The only way to bring it up again is to move to reconsider [36] the vote by which the words were inserted. If the motion to insert is lost, it does not preclude any other motion to insert these words together with other words, or in place of other words, provided the new motion presents essentially new question to the lodge.

To *Strike out Words*. The motion to strike out certain words can be applied only to consecutive words, though, as the result of amendments, the words may be separated when the final vote is taken. If it is desired to strike out separated words, it is necessary to strike out the separated words by separate motions, or still better, a motion may be made to strike out the entire clause or sentence containing the words to be struck out and insert a new clause or sentence as desired. The motion to strike out certain words may be amended only by striking out words from the amendment, the effect of which is to retain in the resolution the words struck out of the amendment provided both motions are adopted. If the motion to strike out certain words is adopted, the same words cannot be again inserted unless the place or the wording is so changed as to make a new proposition. If the motion to strike out fails, it does not preclude a motion to strike out the same words and insert other words, or to strike out a part of the words, or to strike out a part and insert other words; or to strike out these words with others, or to do this and insert other words. In each of these cases the new question is materially different from the old one. For striking out all, or a part, of something that has been previously adopted, see "Rescind, etc." [37].

To *Strike Out* and *Insert Words* is a combination of the two preceding motions, and is indivisible. For purposes of amendment, it is resolved into its constituent elements, and the words to be struck out are first amended, after which the words to be inserted are amended. After their amendment the question is put on the motion to strike out and insert. If it is adopted, the inserted words cannot be struck out, nor can the words struck out be inserted, unless the words or place are so changed as to make the question a new one, as described above. If the motion is lost, it does not preclude either of the single motions to strike out or to insert the same words, nor another motion to strike out and insert, provided there is any material change in either the words to be struck out or the words to be inserted, so that the questions are not practically identical. When it is desired to strike out or modify separated words, a motion may be made to strike out so much of the resolution as is necessary to include all the words to be struck out or changed, and to insert the desired revision including these words. If the words are inserted in the place previously occupied by the words struck out, they may differ materially from the latter, provided they are germane to it. If the words are to be inserted at a different place, then they must not differ materially from those struck out, as it must be in the nature of a transfer. The combined motion to strike out words in one place and to insert different words in another place is not in order. Either the place or the words must be substantially the same. If there are several changes to be made, it is usually better to rewrite the paragraph and offer it as a substitute, as shown further on.

Amendments Affecting an Entire Paragraph. A motion to insert (or add) or to strike out a paragraph, or to substitute one paragraph for another, is an amendment of the first degree, and therefore cannot be made when an amendment is pending. The friends of the paragraph to be inserted or struck out should put it in the best possible shape by amending it before it is voted on. After a paragraph has been inserted it cannot be amended except by adding to it; and it cannot be struck out except in connection with other paragraphs so as to make the question essentially a new one. If a paragraph is struck out, it cannot be inserted afterwards unless it is so changed in wording or place as to present an essentially new question. If the motion to insert or to strike out a paragraph is lost, it does not preclude any other motion except one that presents essentially the same question as the one that the lodge has already decided, as shown above in the case of amending words of a paragraph. Thus, when a motion to insert a paragraph has been lost, it is in order to move to insert a part of the paragraph or the entire paragraph if materially altered. So, though the lodge has refused to strike out a paragraph, it is in order to strike out a part of the paragraph or otherwise to amend it, though it is safer for its friends to make it as nearly perfect as possible before the vote is taken on striking it out, with a view to defeating that motion.

A motion to *substitute* one paragraph for another (which is a combination of the two preceding motions) after being stated by the W. M. is resolved into its two elements for the purpose of amendment, the W. M. at first entertaining amendments only to the paragraph to be struck out, these amendments being of the second degree. After it is perfected by its friends, the W. M. asks if there are any amendments proposed to the paragraph to be inserted. When both paragraphs have been perfected by amendments the question is put on substituting one paragraph for the other. Even though the paragraph constitutes the entire resolution and the motion to substitute is carried, it is necessary afterwards to vote on adopting the resolution, as it has only been voted to substitute one paragraph for another. A paragraph that has been substituted for another cannot be amended afterwards, except by adding to it, like any other paragraph that has been inserted. The paragraph that has been replaced cannot be again inserted unless so modified as to constitute a new question, as with any paragraph that has been struck out. If the motion to substitute is lost, the lodge has only decided that that particular paragraph shall not replace the one specified. It may be willing that it replace some other paragraph, or that it be inserted, or that the paragraph retained in the resolution be further amended, or even struck out. But no amendment is in order that presents to the lodge practically a question that it has already decided.

In parliamentary language it is not correct to speak of "substituting" one word or part of a paragraph for another, as the term is applied to nothing less than a paragraph. When a question is being considered by section, it is in order to move a substitute for the pending section. A substitute for the entire resolution, or report, cannot be moved until the sections have all been considered and the W. M. has announced that the entire paper is open to amendment. When a resolution with amendments of the first and second degree pending, is referred to a committee, they may report it back with a substitute for the resolution which they recommend, even though two amendments are pending. In such a case the W. M. states the question first on the amendments that were pending when the resolution was committed. When they are disposed of, he states the question on the substitute recommended by the committee and proceeds as in case of any other substitute motion.

Improper Amendments. An amendment is not in order which is not germane to the question to be amended; or merely makes the affirmative of the amended question equivalent to the negative of the original question; or is identical with a question previously decided by the lodge during that meeting; or changes one form of amendment to another form; or substitutes one form of motion for another form; or strikes out the word *Resolved* from a resolution; or strikes out or inserts words which would leave no rational proposition before the lodge; or is frivolous or absurd. An amendment of an amendment must be germane to − that is, must relate to − the subject of the amendment as well as the main motion. No independent new question can be introduced under cover of an amendment. But an amendment may be in conflict with the spirit of the original motion and still be germane, and therefore in order.

Illustrations: A resolution of censure may be amended by striking out the word "censure" and inserting the word "thanks," for both relate to opinion of certain conduct; refusing to censure is different from expressing thanks. A resolution to purchase some books could not be amended by striking out the words relating to books and inserting words relating to a building. Suppose a resolution pending directing the treasurer to purchase a desk for the secretary, and an amendment is offered to add the words, "and to pay the expenses of those attending the Grand Lodge Session;" such an amendment is not germane to the resolution, as paying the expenses of the members attending Grand Lodge is in no way related to purchasing a desk for the secretary, and is therefore out of order. But if an amendment were offered to insert the words "and a lodge Minutes Book" after the word "desk," it would be in order, because both are articles to enable the secretary to perform his duties. If a resolution were pending condemning certain things, it could be amended by adding other things that were similar or in some way related to them. Suppose a resolution commending A and B for service is pending; if the acts of service were not connected, amendments are in order adding other names for other acts of service; but if the commendation is for an act of service in which A and B were joined, then no names can be added to the resolution unless the parties were connected with A and B in that act. Suppose the following resolution pending: "*Resolved*, That the Secretary be instructed to notify our real estate agent that we do approve of his desire to search for a new lodge building at a cost of $50,000 higher than originally stated." A motion to amend by inserting "*not*" after the word "*be*" would be out of order, because an affirmative vote on "not instructing" is identical in effect with a negative vote on "instructing." But the motion to insert the word *not* after *do* is in order, for an affirmative vote on disapproving of a certain course is different from a negative vote on a resolution of approval, as the latter may mean nothing but an unwillingness to express an opinion on the subject. Such a motion vote could, however, cause confusion and, while in order, may not be a wise action. If a resolution is pending and a brother makes the motion, "*I move to strike out the words* 'pine benches' *and insert the words* 'oak chairs,'" it is an amendment of the first degree, and no other amendment of that degree is in order until this is acted upon. All the words in italics are necessary for this form of motion, and are not subject to amendment. The only amendments in order are those that change the words "pine benches" or "oak chairs" — that is, first those to be struck out, and when they are perfected, then those to be inserted. Suppose the motion to "*strike out* 'pine'" is pending, and it is moved to amend by adding "*and insert* 'oak.'" This motion is out of order, as it changes one form of amendment to another form. It is not in order to move to strike out the word "adopt" in a motion and insert the word "reject," as "adopt" is a formal word necessary to show the kind of motion made. Practically, however, the same result may be attained by moving to postpone indefinitely — that is, to reject, the main question. The W. M. should never rule an amendment out of order unless he is perfectly sure that it is so. If he is in doubt, he should admit the amendment, or submit the question as to its being in order to the lodge as described in **21**.

Every original main motion may be amended. All others may be amended, except those contained in the following list of motions:

Motions That Cannot Be Amended.

To adjourn or close (except when it is qualified, or when made in a lodge with no provision for a future meeting) **17**
Call for the orders of the day.. **20**
Question of order, and appeal.. **21**
To object to consideration of a question..................................... **23**
Call for a division of the lodge **25**
To grant leave to withdraw a motion **27**
To grant leave to speak after indecorum..................................... **21**
A request of any kind.. **27**
To take up a question out of its proper order.............................. **22**
To suspend the rules.. **22**
To lay on the table **28**
To take from the table **35**
To reconsider **36**
The previous question... **29**
To postpone indefinitely **34**
To amend an amendment **33**
To fill a blank.. **33**
A nomination **64**

A motion to adopt a resolution or a bylaw may be amended by adding, "and that it be printed and that brothers be supplied with copies," or, "that they go into effect at the close of this meeting," or anything of a similar kind. Under each of the privileged, incidental, and subsidiary motions, it is stated whether or not the motion may be amended, and, when necessary, the way in which it may be amended is explained. An amendment to anything already adopted is not a subsidiary motion. The matter to be amended is not pending and is therefore not affected by anything done with the amendment, provided it is not adopted. Such an amendment is a main motion subject to amendments of the first and second degrees. If the motion is to strike out an entire resolution that has been adopted, it is usually called to *Rescind* and is explained under that head [37]. If the motion is to amend a by-law, etc., it will be found under Amendments of Constitutions, Bylaws, etc. [66]. Minutes are usually amended (corrected) informally, the W. M. directing the correction to be made when suggested. But if objection is made, a formal vote is necessary for the amendment. The minutes may be corrected whenever the error is noticed regardless of the time which has elapsed; but after their adoption, when too late to reconsider the vote, they require a two-thirds vote for their amendment, unless previous notice of the proposed amendment has been given, when only a majority vote is required for its adoption, the same as with the motion to rescind [37]. This is necessary for the protection of the records, which otherwise would be subject to the risk of being tampered with by temporary majorities. The numbers prefixed to paragraphs, articles, etc., are only marginal indications and should be corrected by the secretary, if necessary, without any motion to amend. For amending a long paper, such as a series of resolutions, or a set of bylaws, which should be considered and amended by paragraph, see **24**.

Filling Blanks. Propositions for filling blanks are treated somewhat differently from other amendments, in that any number of brothers may propose, without a second, different names or numbers for filling the blanks, no one proposing more than one name or number for each place, unless by general consent. These are treated not as amendments, one of another, but as independent propositions to be voted on successively. If the blank is to be filled with a name, the W. M. repeats the names as they are proposed so all may hear them, and finally takes a vote on each name, beginning with the first proposed, until one receives a majority vote. If the blank is to be filled with several names and no more names are suggested than required, the names may be inserted without a vote. If more names than required are suggested, a vote is taken on each, beginning with the first, until enough to fill the blank have received a majority vote. If the number of names is not specified, a vote is taken on each name suggested, and all that receive a majority vote are inserted.

If the blank is to be filled with a number or a date, then the largest sum, or the longest time, or the most distant date, is put first, unless it is evident to the W. M. that the reverse order is necessary to enable the first vote to be taken on the proposition that is least likely to be adopted. Suppose a committee is being instructed to purchase a building for a blank amount: the voting on filling the blank should begin with the largest sum proposed; if that is lost, all who voted for it, and some others, would favor the next largest sum, so that the vote would be greater, and so on down to the largest sum that is favored by a majority. If the voting began with the smallest sum, everyone would be willing to pay that amount, and it might be adopted and thus cut off voting on the other propositions, whereas a majority would prefer authorizing the committee to spend a larger amount. On the other hand, suppose the committee was being authorized to sell a building for a blank amount: here it is evident that there would be more in favor of the large sum than of the small one. So, to get at the wish of the lodge the voting should begin with the smallest sum proposed; all who are willing to sell for that amount, and some additional ones, will be willing to sell for the next larger sum; and so, the smallest sum for which the majority is willing to sell will be gradually reached.

It is sometimes convenient to create a blank, as in the following example: A resolution is pending requesting the lodge be moved to a building on A street, and an amendment to strike out A and insert B, and an amendment of the second degree to strike out B and insert C, have been made. The debate developing the fact that several other streets have their advocates, the best course is for the W. M. to state that, if there is no objection, the motion would be treated as having a blank for the name of the street, and that A, B, and C have been proposed for filling the blank. In this way other names could be suggested, and they would be voted on successively beginning with the first street suggested, and continuing down until one was reached that could get a majority in its favor. If objection is made to leaving a blank for the name, the W. M. may put the question without waiting for a motion, or anyone may move, as an incidental motion, that a blank be created for the name of the street. This motion is undebatable, and cannot be amended, but it may be moved to fill the blank by ballot or in any other way.

The blanks in a resolution should be filled usually before voting on the resolution. But sometimes, when a large majority is opposed to the resolution, the previous question is ordered without waiting for the blanks to be filled, thus stopping debate and further amendment, and bringing the lodge at once to a vote on the resolution. Under such circumstances the resolution would usually be rejected. But should it be adopted; it would be necessary to fill the blanks in the skeleton resolution before any other than privileged business would be in order.

The method adopted in filling blanks has sometimes a great advantage over ordinary amendment. In amending, the last one proposed is the first one voted on, whereas in filling blanks the first one proposed, or nominated, is voted on first, except where, from the nature of the case, another order is preferable, and then that order is adopted as explained above.

Nominations are treated like filling blanks; any number may be pending at the same time, not as amendments of each other, but as independent propositions to be voted on in the order in which they were made until one receives a majority vote. [See **64**.]

34. To Postpone Indefinitely

To Postpone Indefinitely takes precedence of nothing except the main motion to which it is applied, and yields to all privileged [**14**], incidental [**13**], and other subsidiary [**12**] motions. It cannot be amended or have any other subsidiary motion applied to it except the previous question and motions limiting or extending the limits of debate. It is debatable and opens the main question to debate. It can be applied to nothing but main questions, which include questions of privilege and orders of the day after they are before the lodge for consideration. An affirmative vote on it may be reconsidered, but not a negative vote. If lost it cannot be renewed. It is simply a motion to reject the main question. If a main motion is referred to a committee while to postpone indefinitely is pending, the latter motion is ignored and does not go to the committee.

The *Object* of this motion is not to postpone, but to reject, the main motion without incurring the risk of a direct vote on it, and it is made only by the enemies of the main motion when they are in doubt as to their being in the majority.

The *Effect* of making this motion is to enable brothers who have exhausted their right of debate on the main question, to speak again, as technically, the question before the lodge is different, while, as far as the subject of discussion is concerned, there is no difference caused by changing the question from adopting to rejecting the measure, because the merits of the main question are open to debate in either case. If adopted, its effect is to suppress the main motion for that meeting, unless the vote is reconsidered. As this motion does not suppress the debate on the main question, its only useful effect is to give the opponents of the pending measure a chance of killing the main motion without risking its adoption in case of failure. For, if they carry the indefinite postponement, the main question is suppressed for the meeting; if they fail, they still have a vote on the main question, and, having learned their strength by the vote taken, they can form an opinion of the advisability of continuing the struggle.

Art. VI

Some Main and Unclassified Motions.

35. To Take from the Table

To Take from the Table takes precedence of no pending question, but has the right of way in preference to main motions if made during the meeting in which it was laid on the table while no question is actually pending, and at a time when business of this class, or unfinished business, or new business, is in order; and also, during the next meeting in societies having regular business meetings as frequently as quarterly. It yields to privileged [14] and incidental [13] motions, but not to subsidiary [12] ones. It is undebatable, and no subsidiary motion can be applied to it. It is not in order unless some business has been transacted since the question was laid on the table, nor can it be renewed until some business has been transacted since it was lost The motion to take from the table cannot be reconsidered, as it can be renewed repeatedly if lost, and, if carried, the question can be again laid on the table after progress in debate or business.

In lodges, a question is supposed to be laid on the table only temporarily with the expectation of its consideration being resumed after the disposal of the interrupting question, or at a more convenient season. As soon as the question that was introduced when the first question was laid on the table, is disposed of, anyone may move to take this first question from the table. When he rises to make the motion, if the W. M. recognizes someone else as having first risen, he should at once say that he rises to move to take a question from the table. The W. M. then assigns him the floor if the other brother has risen to make a main motion. If the new main motion has been stated by the W. M. before he claims the floor, he must wait until that question is disposed of before his motion will be in order. When taken up, the question with everything adhering to it is before the lodge exactly as when it was laid on the table. Thus, if a resolution has amendments and a motion to commit pending at the time it was laid on the table, when it is taken from the table the question is first on the motion to commit. If a motion to postpone to a certain time is pending when the question is laid on the table, and it is taken from the table after that time, then the motion to postpone is ignored when the question is taken up. If the question is taken up on the day it was laid on the table, brothers who have exhausted their right of debate cannot again speak on the question. But if taken up on another day, no notice is taken of speeches previously made. The previous question is not exhausted if the question upon which it was ordered is taken from the table at the same meeting, even though it is on another day.

36. Reconsider.

This motion is peculiar in that the making of the motion has a higher rank than its consideration, and for a certain time prevents anything being done as the result of the vote it is proposed to reconsider. It can be made only on the day the vote to be reconsidered was taken, or on the next succeeding meeting. It must be made by one who voted with the prevailing side. Any brother may second it. It can be made while any other question is pending, even if another brother has the floor. It may be made after the previous question has been ordered, in which case it and the motion to be reconsidered are undebatable.

While the making of the motion to reconsider has such high privilege, its consideration has only the rank of the motion to be reconsidered, though it has the right of way in preference to any new motion of equal rank, as illustrated further on; and the reconsideration of a vote disposing of a main question either temporarily or permanently may be called up, when no question is pending, even though the general orders are being carried out. The motion to reconsider cannot be amended, postponed indefinitely, or committed. If the reconsideration is laid on the table or postponed definitely, the question to be reconsidered and all adhering questions go with it. The previous question and the motions limiting or extending the limits of debate may be applied to it when it is debatable. It is undebatable only when the motion to be reconsidered is undebatable. When debatable it opens to debate the merits of the question to be reconsidered. It cannot be withdrawn after it is too late to renew the motion. If the motion to reconsider is lost it cannot be repeated except by general consent. No question can be twice reconsidered unless it was materially amended after its first reconsideration. A reconsideration requires only a majority vote, regardless of the vote necessary to adopt the motion reconsidered.

The motion to reconsider *cannot be applied* to a vote on a motion that may be renewed within a reasonable time; or when practically the same result may be attained by some other parliamentary motion; or when the vote has been partially executed (except in case of the motion to limit debate), or something has been done as the result of the vote that the lodge cannot undo; or to an affirmative vote in the nature of a contract, when the other party to the contract has been notified of the vote; or to a vote on the motion to reconsider. In accordance with these principles, votes on the following motions *cannot be reconsidered*: Lay on the Table; Take from the Table; Suspend the Rules or Order of Business; and Reconsider. Affirmative votes on the following cannot be reconsidered: Proceed to the Orders of the Day; Adopt, or after they are adopted, to Amend, or Repeal, or Rescind, the Constitution, Bylaws, or Rules of Order or any other rules that require previous notice for their amendment; Elect to office if the brother or officer is present and does not decline, or if absent and has learned of his election in the usual way and has not declined; to Reopen Nominations. A negative vote on the motion to Postpone Indefinitely cannot be reconsidered as practically the same question comes up again when the vote is taken on the main question. After a committee has taken up the matter referred to it, it is too late to reconsider the vote committing it, though the committee may be discharged. But after debate has proceeded under an order limiting or extending the limits of debate, the vote making that order may be reconsidered, as the debate may develop facts that make it desirable to return to the regular rules of debate. The minutes, or record of proceedings, may be corrected at any time without reconsidering the vote approving them.

If the main question is pending and it is moved to reconsider the vote on any subsidiary [12], incidental [13], or privileged [14] motion, the W. M. states the question on the reconsideration the moment the motion to be reconsidered is in order if it were made then for the first time. Thus, if, while the motions to commit, for the previous question, and to lay on the table are pending, it is moved to reconsider a negative vote on postponing to a certain time, the W. M.

proceeds to take the vote on laying on the table and, if that is lost, next on the previous question, and then on reconsidering the vote on the postponement, and if that is adopted, then on the postponement, and if that is lost, then on to commit. If the motion to lay on the table had been carried, then when the question was taken from the table the same method of procedure would be followed; that is, the question would be first on ordering the previous question, and next on reconsidering the vote on the postponement, etc. If the reconsideration of an amendment of the first degree is moved while another amendment of the same degree is pending, the pending amendment is first disposed of and then the W. M. announces the question on the reconsideration of the amendment. If the reconsideration of an amendment to an immediately pending question is moved the W. M. at once announces the question on the reconsideration.

If the reconsideration is moved while another subject is before the lodge, it cannot interrupt the pending business, but, as soon as that has been disposed of, if called up it has the preference over all other main motions and general orders. In such a case the W. M. does not state the question on the reconsideration until it is called up.

If the motion to reconsider is made at a time when the reconsideration could be called up if it had been previously made, the W. M. at once states the question on the reconsideration, unless the mover adds to his motion the words, "and have it entered on the minutes," as explained further on.

If, after the vote has been taken on the adoption of a main motion, it is desired to consider the vote on an amendment, it is necessary to reconsider the vote on the main question also, and one motion should be made to cover both votes. The same principle applies in case of an amendment to an amendment, whether the vote has been taken on the resolution, or only on the amendment of the first degree. When the motion covers the reconsideration of two or three votes, the debate is limited to the question that was first voted on. Thus, if the motion is to reconsider the votes on a resolution and amendments of the first and second degree, the debate is limited to the amendment of the second degree. If the motion to reconsider is adopted the W. M. states the question on the amendment of the second degree and recognizes the mover of the reconsideration as entitled to the floor. The question is now in exactly the same condition it was in just previous to taking the original vote on that amendment.

The *Forms* of making this motion are as follows: "I move to reconsider the vote on the resolution relating to a banquet." "I move to reconsider the vote on the amendment to strike out 'Wednesday' and insert 'Thursday.'" [This form is used when the resolution is still pending.] "I move to reconsider the votes on the resolution relating to a banquet and on the amendment to strike out 'Wednesday' and insert 'Thursday'" [This form is used when the vote has been taken on the resolution, and it is desired to reconsider the vote on an amendment.] When the motion to reconsider is made the W. M. states the question, if it can then be considered, and proceeds as with any other question. If it cannot be considered at that time, he says, "Br. A moves to reconsider the vote on.... The secretary will make a note of it," and proceeds with the pending business. The reconsideration, after being moved, is brought before the lodge for action as explained in the previous paragraph. If it is *called up* by a brother, he simply says, after obtaining the floor, "I call up the motion to reconsider the vote on ..." This call requires no second or vote. If the call is in order, as previously explained, the W. M. says, "The motion to reconsider the vote [or votes] on ... is called up. The question is, 'Will the lodge reconsider the vote [or votes] on ...? Are you ready for the question?'" If the reconsideration is one that the W. M. states the question on as soon as it can be considered (as when it is moved to reconsider an amendment while another amendment is pending), as soon as the proper time arrives the W. M. states the question on the reconsideration the same as if the motion to reconsider were made at this time.

When the debate, if there is any, is finished, he *puts the question* thus: "As many as are in favor of reconsidering the vote on the resolution relating to a banquet, say *aye*; those opposed say *no*. The ayes have it and the vote on the resolution is reconsidered. The question is now on the resolution, which is," etc. Or the question may be put thus: "The question is, Will the lodge reconsider the votes on the resolution relating to a banquet, and on the amendment to strike out 'Wednesday' and insert 'Thursday?' As many as are in favor of the reconsideration say *aye*; those opposed say *no*. The ayes have it and the votes on the resolution and the amendment are reconsidered. The question is now on the amendment, which is," etc. If the motion to reconsider is adopted the business is in exactly the same condition it was in before taking the vote, or the votes, that have been reconsidered, and the W. M. instantly states the question on the immediately pending question, which is then open to debate and amendment as before.

The *Effect of Making* this motion is to suspend all action that the original motion would have required until the reconsideration is acted upon; but if it is not called up, this effect terminates with the meeting. As long as its effect lasts, any one at an adjourned, or a special, or a regular meeting, may *call up* the motion to reconsider and have it acted upon, though it is not usual for anyone but the mover to call it up on the day it is made if the meeting lasts beyond that day and there is no need of prompt action.

The *Effect of the Adoption* of this motion is to place before the lodge the original question in the exact position it occupied before it was voted upon; consequently no one, after the reconsideration is adopted, can debate the question reconsidered who had on that day exhausted his right of debate on that question; his only recourse is to discuss the question while the motion to reconsider is before the lodge. If the question is not reconsidered until a later day than that on which the vote to be reconsidered was taken, then it is open to free debate regardless of speeches made previously. When a vote taken under the operation of the previous question is reconsidered, the question is then divested of the previous question, and is open to debate and amendment, provided the previous question had been exhausted by votes taken on all the questions covered by it, before the motion to reconsider was made.

In standing and special committees, a vote may be reconsidered regardless of the time elapsed since the vote was taken, provided the motion is made by one who did not vote with the losing side, and that all brothers who voted with the prevailing side are present, or have received due notice that the reconsideration would be moved at this meeting. A vote cannot be reconsidered in committee of the whole.

Reconsider and Have Entered on the Minutes. The motion to reconsider, as previously explained in this section, provides means for correcting, at least on the day on which it occurred, errors due to hasty action. By using the same motion and having it entered on the minutes so that it cannot be called up until another day, a means is provided for preventing a temporary majority from taking action that is opposed by the majority of the lodge. This is needed in large lodges with frequent meetings and small quorums. It enables a society with a small quorum to protect itself from injudicious action by temporary majorities, without requiring previous notice of main motions and amendments as is done in the English Parliament. To accomplish this, however, it is necessary to allow this form of the motion to be applied to a vote finally disposing of a main motion, regardless of the fact that the motion to reconsider has already been made. Otherwise, it would be useless, as it would generally be forestalled by the motion to reconsider, in its simple form, which would be voted down, and then this motion could not be made. As this form of the motion is designed only to be used when the meeting is an unrepresentative one, this fact should be very apparent, and some brothers of the temporary minority should vote with the temporary majority on adopting or postponing indefinitely a main motion of importance, when they think the action is in opposition to the wishes of the great majority of the lodge. One of them should then move "to reconsider the vote on the resolution [or motion] and have it [or, request that it be] entered on the minutes," which has the effect of suspending all action required by the vote it is proposed to reconsider, as previously explained, and thus gives time to notify absent brothers of the proposed action. If no brother of the temporary minority voted with the majority, and it is too late for anyone to change his vote so as to move to reconsider, then someone should give notice of a motion to rescind the objectionable vote at the next meeting, which may be done by a majority vote after this notice has been given.

Should a minority make an improper use of this form of the motion to reconsider by applying it to a vote which required action before the next regular business meeting, the remedy is at once to vote that when the lodge adjourns it adjourns to meet on another day, appointing a suitable day, when the reconsideration could be called up and disposed of. The mere making of this motion would probably cause the withdrawal of the motion to reconsider, as it would defeat the object of that motion if the majority of the lodge is in favor of the motion to be reconsidered. If the motion to reconsider is withdrawn, of course the other would be.

This form of the motion to reconsider and have entered on the minutes differs from the simple form to reconsider in the following respects:

(1) It can be made only on the day the vote to be reconsidered is taken. If a meeting is held on the next day the simple form of the motion to reconsider, made then, accomplishes the object of this motion by bringing the question before the lodge on a different day from the one when the vote was taken.

(2) It outranks the simple form of the motion to reconsider, and may be made even after the vote has been taken on the motion to reconsider, provided the result of the vote has not been announced. If made after the simple form of the motion to reconsider, it supersedes the latter, which is thereafter ignored.

(3) It can be applied only to votes which finally dispose of the main question. They are as follows: an affirmative or negative vote on adapting, and an affirmative vote on postponing indefinitely, a main question. And it may be applied to a negative vote on the consideration of a question that has been objected to.

(4) It cannot be called up on the day it is made.

After it is called up there is no difference in the treatment of the two forms of the motion.

37. Rescind, Repeal, or Annul.

Any vote taken by a lodge, except those mentioned further on, may be rescinded by a majority vote, provided notice of the motion has been given at the previous meeting or in the call for this meeting; or it may be rescinded without notice by a two-thirds vote, or by a vote of a majority of the entire membership. The notice may be given when another question is pending, but cannot interrupt a brother while speaking. To rescind is identical with the motion to amend something previously adopted, by striking out the entire bylaw, rule, resolution, section, or paragraph, and is subject to all the limitations as to notice and vote that may be placed by the rules on similar amendments. It is a main motion without any privilege, and therefore can be introduced only when there is nothing else before the lodge. It cannot be made if the question can be reached by calling up the motion to reconsider which has been previously made. It may be made by any brother; it is debatable and yields to all privileged and incidental motions; and all of the subsidiary motions may be applied to it. The motion to rescind can be applied to votes on all main motions, including questions of privilege and orders of the day that have been acted upon, and to votes on an appeal, with the following *exceptions*: votes cannot be rescinded after something has been done as a result of that vote that the lodge cannot undo; or where it is in the nature of a contract and the other party is informed of the fact; or, where a resignation has been acted upon, or one has been elected to, or expelled from, membership or office, and was present or has been officially notified.

Where it is desired not only to rescind the action, but to express very strong disapproval, legislative bodies have, on rare occasions, voted to rescind the objectionable resolution and *expunge* it from the record, which is done by crossing out the words, or drawing a line around them, and writing across them the words, "Expunged by order of the lodge," etc., giving the date of the order. This statement should be signed by the secretary. The words expunged must not be so blotted as not to be readable, as otherwise it would be impossible to determine whether more was expunged than ordered. Any vote less than a majority of the total membership of an organization is certainly incompetent to expunge from the records a correct statement of what was done and recorded and the record of which was officially approved, even though a quorum is present and the vote to expunge is unanimous.

38. Renewal of a Motion.

When an original main motion or an amendment has been adopted, or rejected, or a main motion has been postponed indefinitely, or an objection to its consideration has been sustained, it, or practically the same motion, cannot be again brought before the lodge at the same meeting, except by a motion to reconsider or to rescind the vote. But it may be introduced again at any future meeting.

In lodges or bodies having regular meetings as often at least as monthly, a main motion cannot be renewed until after the close of the next regular meeting, if it was postponed to that next meeting; or laid on the table; or adopted, or rejected, or postponed indefinitely, and the motion to reconsider was made and not acted on at the previous meeting. In these cases, the question can be reached at the next meeting at the time to which it was postponed, or by taking it from the table, or by reconsidering the vote.

In lodges or bodies whose regular meetings are not as frequent as quarterly, any motion which has not been committed or postponed to the next meeting may be renewed at that next meeting. The motion to lay on the table, may be made again and again, provided there has been progress in debate or business, but the making of, or voting on, this motion is not business that justifies the renewal of a motion. Neither a motion to postpone indefinitely nor an amendment can be renewed at the same meeting, but other subsidiary motions may be renewed whenever the progress in debate or business is such as to make the question before the lodge practically a different one. To take from the table and a call for the orders of the day may be renewed after the business is disposed of that was taken up when the motion to take from the table, or for the orders of the day, was lost. To postpone indefinitely cannot be renewed even though the main motion has been amended since the indefinite postponement was previously moved. A point of order cannot be raised if an identical one has been raised previously without success during the same meeting. And after the W. M. has given a ruling, he need not entertain an appeal from a similar decision during the same meeting. Minutes may be corrected regardless of the time elapsed and of the fact that the correction had been previously proposed and lost.

When a subject which has been referred to a committee is reported back at the same meeting, or a subject that has been laid on the table is taken up at the same meeting, it is not a renewal.

The following motions, unless they have been withdrawn, *cannot be renewed* at the same meeting: to adopt or postpone indefinitely an original main motion; to amend; to reconsider, unless the question to be reconsidered was amended materially when previously reconsidered; to object to the consideration of a question; to fix the same time to which to adjourn; to suspend the rules for the same purpose at the same meeting, though it may be renewed at another meeting held the same day.

It is the duty of the W. M. to prevent the privilege of renewal from being used to obstruct business, and when it is evident that it is being so misused he should protect the lodge by refusing to recognize the motions, as explained under Dilatory Motions [40].

39. Ratify.

This is a main motion and is used when it is desired to confirm or make valid some action which requires the approval of the lodge to make it valid. The lodge may ratify only such actions of its officers or committees, or delegates, as it had the right to authorize in advance. It cannot make valid a viva voce election when the bylaws require it to be by ballot, nor can it ratify anything done in violation of the laws of the state, the Grand Lodge, or of its own bylaws.

40. Dilatory, Absurd, or Frivolous Motions.

For the convenience of lodges, it is necessary to allow some highly privileged motions to be renewed again and again after progress in debate or the transaction of any business, and to allow a single brother, by calling for a division, to have another vote taken. If there was no provision for protecting the lodge, a minority of two brothers could be constantly raising questions of order, and calling for a division on every vote, even when it was nearly unanimous, and moving to lay motions on the table, and offering amendments that are simply frivolous or absurd. By taking advantage of parliamentary forms and methods a small minority could practically stop the business of a lodge having short meetings, if there was no provision for such contingency. Congress met it by adopting this rule: "No dilatory motion shall be entertained by the speaker." But, without adopting any rule on the subject, every lodge has the inherent right to protect itself from being imposed upon by brothers using parliamentary forms to prevent it from doing the very thing for which it is in meeting, and which these forms were designed to assist, namely, to transact business. Therefore, whenever the W. M. is satisfied that brothers are using parliamentary forms merely to obstruct business, he should either not recognize them, or else rule them out of order. After the W. M. has so acted, he should not entertain another appeal from the same obstructionists while they are engaged evidently in trying by that means to obstruct business. While the W. M. should always be courteous and fair, he should be firm in protecting the lodge from imposition, even though it be done in strict conformity with all parliamentary rules except this one, that no dilatory, absurd, or frivolous motions are allowed.

As an illustration of a frivolous or absurd motion, suppose Br. A is to be in the city next month and a motion has been made to invite him to address the lodge at its next meeting, the lodge meeting monthly. Now, if a motion is made to refer the question to a committee with instructions to report at the next regular meeting, the W. M. should rule it out of order as frivolous or absurd.

41. Summons.

The object of a Summons is to compel the attendance of brothers at lodge for reasons stated in the Summons. A Summons may be issued in the case of a Masonic trial, but may be issued for any cause at the will of the Worshipful Master. In most cases, a Summons is sent out by the Secretary and under the seal of the lodge. In some jurisdictions, failure to answer a Summons is grounds for Masonic charges in many jurisdictions.

Art. VII

Debate

42. Debate
43. Decorum in Debate
44. Closing and Preventing Debate
45. Principles of Debate and Undebatable Motions

42. Debate.

In **1-6** are explained the necessary steps preliminary to debate namely, that when no business is pending a brother shall rise and address the W. M. by his title, and be recognized by the W. M. as having obtained the floor; and that the brother shall then make a motion which, after being seconded, shall be stated by the W. M., who shall then ask, "Are you ready for the question?" The question is then open to debate, as is partially explained in **7**, which should be read in connection with this section. No brother shall speak more than twice during the same day to the same question (only once on an appeal), nor longer than ten minutes at one time, without leave of the Worshipful Master. No brother can speak a second time to a question as long as any brother desires to speak who has not spoken to the question. If greater freedom is desired, the proper course is to go into committee of the whole, or to consider it informally, either of which requires only a majority vote; or to extend the limits of debate [**30**], which requires a two-thirds vote. So, the debate, by a two-thirds vote, may be limited to any extent desired, as shown in **30**. The brother upon whose motion the subject was brought before the lodge, is entitled to close the debate with a speech, if he has not previously exhausted his twenty minutes, but not until everyone else wishing to speak has spoken. He cannot, however, avail himself of this privilege after debate has been closed. An amendment, or any other motion, being offered, makes the real question before the lodge a different one, and, in regard to the right to debate, is treated as a new question. When an amendment is pending the debate must be confined to the merits of the amendment, unless it is of such a nature that its decision practically decides the main question. Merely asking a question, or making a suggestion, is not considered as speaking. The maker of a motion, though he can vote against it, cannot speak against his own motion. [To close the debate, see **44**.]

The right of brothers to debate and, make motions cannot be cut off by the W. M.'s putting a question to vote with such rapidity as to prevent the brothers getting the floor after the W. M. has inquired if the lodge is ready for the question. Even after the W. M. has announced the vote, if it is found that a brother arose and addressed the W. M. with reasonable promptness after the W. M.

asked, "Are you ready for the question?" he is then entitled to the floor, and the question is in exactly the same condition it was before it was put to vote. But if the W. M. gives ample opportunity for brothers to claim the floor before putting the question and they do not avail themselves of it, they cannot claim the right of debate after the voting has commenced.

43. Decorum in Debate.

In debate a brother must confine himself to the question before the lodge, and avoid personalities. He cannot reflect upon any act of the lodge, unless he intends to conclude his remarks with a motion to rescind such action, or else while debating such a motion. In referring to another brother, he should, as much as possible, avoid using his name, rather referring to him as "the brother who spoke last," or in some other way describing him. The officers of the lodge or visiting officers should always be referred to by their Masonic titles. It is not allowable to arraign the motives of a brother, but the nature or consequences of a measure may be condemned in strong terms. It is not the man, but the measure, which is the subject of debate.

If one desires to ask a question of the brother speaking, he should rise, and say, "W. M., I should like to ask the brother a question." The W. M. then asks the speaker if he is willing to be interrupted, or the speaker may at once consent or decline, addressing, however, the W. M., through whom the conversation must be carried on, as brothers should not directly address one another during a debate. If the speaker consents to the question, the time consumed by the interruption comes out of the time of the speaker.

If at any time the W. M. rises to state a point of order, or give information, or otherwise speak, within his privilege, the brother speaking must take his seat till the W. M. has been heard first. When called to order by the W. M. the brother must sit down until the question of order is decided.

During debate, and while the W. M. is speaking, or the lodge is engaged in voting, no brother is permitted to disturb the lodge by whispering, or walking across the floor, or in any other way.

44. Closing and Preventing Debate.

When the debate appears to the W. M. to be finished, he should inquire, "Are you ready for the question?" If, after a reasonable pause, no one rises to claim the floor, the W. M. assumes that no brother wishes to speak and proceeds to put the question. Debate is not closed by the W. M.'s putting the question, as until both the affirmative and the negative are put, a brother can rise and claim the floor, and reopen the debate or make a motion, provided he rises with reasonable promptness after the W. M. asks, "Are you ready for the question?" If the debate is resumed the question must be put again, both the affirmative and the negative. Should this privilege be abused by brothers not responding to the inquiry, "Are you ready for the question?" and intentionally waiting until the affirmative vote has been taken and then rising and reopening the debate, the W. M. should act as in case of dilatory motions [40], or any other attempt to obstruct business, and protect the lodge from annoyance. When a vote is taken a second time, as when a division is called for, debate cannot be resumed except by general consent.

45. Principles of Debate and Undebatable Motions.

All main motions are debatable, and debate is allowed or prohibited on other motions in accordance with the following principles:

(a) High privilege is, as a rule, incompatible with the right of debate of the privileged motion: and, therefore, all highly privileged motions are undebatable, except those relating to the privileges of the lodge or a brother. Questions of privilege [19] rarely arise, but when they do, they are likely to be so important that they must be allowed to interrupt business, and yet they cannot generally be acted upon intelligently without debate and, therefore, they are debatable.

(b) Motions that have the effect of suspending a rule are not debatable. Consequently, motions to suppress, or to limit, or to extend the limits of, debate are undebatable, as they suspend the ordinary rules of debate.

(c) Appeals made after the previous question has been ordered are undebatable, as it would be manifestly improper to permit debate on them when the lodge by a two-thirds vote has closed debate on the pending question. So, any order limiting debate on the pending question applies to questions arising while the order is in force.

(d) To Amend, or to Reconsider, an undebatable question is undebatable, whereas to amend, or to reconsider, a debatable question is debatable.

(e) A Subsidiary Motion [12] is debatable to just the extent that it interferes with the right of the lodge to take up the original question at its pleasure. *Illustrations*: To "Postpone Indefinitely" a question places it out of the power of the lodge to again take it up during that meeting, except by reconsideration, and consequently this motion allows of free debate, even involving the whole merits of the original question. To "Commit" a question only delays the discussion until the committee reports, when it is open to free debate, so it is only debatable as to the propriety of the commitment and as to the instructions, etc. To "Postpone to a Certain Time" prevents the consideration of the question till the specified time, except by a reconsideration or suspension of the rules, and therefore allows of limited debate upon the propriety of the postponement. To "Lay on the Table" leaves the question so that the lodge can consider it at any time that that question or that class of business is in order, and therefore to lay on the table should not be, and is not, debatable.

Because a motion is undebatable it does not follow that while it is pending the W. M. may not permit a question or an explanation. The distinction between debate and asking questions or making brief suggestions, should be kept clearly in mind, and when the latter will aid the lodge in transacting business, the W. M. should permit it before taking the vote on an undebatable question.

The following lists of motions that open the main question to debate, and of those that are undebatable, are made in accordance with the above principles:

Motions That Open the Main Question to Debate.

Undebatable Motions.

Art. VIII

Vote

46. Voting.

If the question is undebatable, or debate has been closed, the W. M., immediately after stating the question, puts it to vote as described under Putting the Question [9], only allowing time for brothers to rise if they wish to make a motion of higher rank.

If the question is debatable and no one rises to claim the floor, after the question is stated by the W. M., he should inquire, "Are you ready for the question?" After a moment's pause, if no one rises, he should put the question to vote. If the question is debated or motions are made, the W. M. should wait until the debate has apparently ceased, when he should again inquire, "Are you ready for the question?" Having given ample time for anyone to rise and claim the floor, and no one having done so, he should put the question to vote and announce the result.

The usual method of taking a vote is *viva voce* (by the voice). The rules require this method to be used in Congress. In small lodges the vote is often taken by "show of hands," or by "raising the right hand" as it is also called. The other methods of voting are by rising; by ballot; by roll call, and by "yeas and nays," as it is also called. In voting, the affirmative answer *aye*, or raise the right hand, or rise, as the case may be: then the negative answer *no*, or raise the right hand, or rise.

The responsibility of announcing, or declaring, the vote rests upon the W.M., and he, therefore, has the right to have the vote taken again, by rising, if he is in doubt as to the result, and even to have the vote counted, if necessary. He cannot have the vote taken by ballot or by yeas and nays (roll call) unless it is required by the rules or by a vote of the lodge. But if the *viva voce* vote does not make him positive as to the result he may at once say, "Those in favor of the motion will rise;" and when they are seated, he will continue, "Those opposed will rise." If this does not enable him to determine the vote, he should say, "Those in favor of the motion [or, Those in the affirmative] will rise and stand until counted." He then counts those standing, or directs the secretary to do so, and then says, "Be seated. Those opposed [or, Those in the negative] rise and stand until counted." After both sides are counted the W. M. announces the result as shown below. In a very large lodge, the W. M. may find it necessary to appoint tellers to count the vote and report to him the numbers. In small lodges a show of hands may be substituted for a rising vote.

When the vote is taken by voice or show of hands any brother has a right to request a *division of the lodge* [25] by having the affirmative rise and then the negative, so that all may see how brothers vote. Either before or after a decision any brother may call for, or demand, a count, and, if seconded, the W. M. must put the question on ordering a count.

Announcing the Vote. When the vote has been taken so that the W. M. has no doubt as to the result, and no division is called for, or, if so, the lodge has divided, the W. M. proceeds to announce, or declare the vote thus: "The ayes have it and the resolution is adopted." If the vote was by show of hands or by rising, it would be announced thus: "The affirmative has it (or the motion is carried) and the question is laid on the table;" or if there was a count, the vote would be announced thus: "There are 25 votes in the affirmative, and 29 in the negative, so the amendment is lost, and the question is now on the resolution; are you ready for the question?" In announcing a vote, the W. M. should state first whether the motion is carried or lost; second, what is the effect, or result, of the vote; and third, what is the immediately pending question or business, if there is any. If there is none, he should ask, "What is the further pleasure of the lodge?" One of the most prolific causes of confusion in lodges is the neglect of the W. M. to keep the lodge well informed as to what is the pending business. The habit of announcing the vote by simply saying that the "motion is carried," cannot be too strongly condemned. Many brothers may not know what the effect of the vote is, and it is the W. M.'s duty to inform the lodge what is the result of the motion's being carried or lost, and what business comes next before the lodge.

In the event of a tie, the W.M. should cast his vote so that the tie may be broken.

It is a general rule that no one should vote on a question in which he has a direct personal or pecuniary interest. Yet this does not prevent a brother from voting for himself for any office or other position. If a brother could in no case vote on a question affecting himself, it would be impossible for a lodge to vote to hold a banquet, or to vote on the payment of a bill (or services rendered) by the brother. A sense of delicacy usually prevents a brother from exercising this right of voting in matters affecting himself except where his vote might affect the result.

A brother has the right to change his vote up to the time the vote is finally announced. After that, he can make the change only by permission of the W.M. and consent of the lodge, which may be given by general consent; that is, by no brother's objecting when the W. M. inquires if anyone objects. If objection is made, a motion may be made to grant the permission, which motion is undebatable.

While it is the duty of every brother who has an opinion on the question to express it by his vote, yet he cannot be compelled to do so. He may prefer to abstain from voting, though he knows the effect is the same as if he voted on the prevailing side. Many lodges require all members to vote if the vote is on the admission of a candidate. In such cases, no member present may abstain from casting his vote.

Voting by Ballot. The main object of this form of voting is secrecy, and it is resorted to when the question is of such a nature that some brothers might hesitate to vote publicly their true sentiments. Its special use is in elections, admission of candidates and trials, and the bylaws should require the vote to be by ballot in such cases. Where the bylaws do not require the vote to be by ballot, it can be so ordered by a majority vote, general consent, or by the Worshipful Master. Such motions are undebatable. As the usual object of the ballot is secrecy, where the bylaws require the vote to be taken by ballot any motion is out of order which brothers cannot oppose without exposing their views on the question to be decided by ballot. Thus, it is out of order to move that one person cast the ballot of the lodge for a certain person when the bylaws require the vote to be by ballot. So, when the ballot is not unanimous it is out of order to move to make the vote unanimous, unless the motion is voted on by ballot so as to allow brothers to vote against it in secrecy.

In some cases, black balls (many times black *cubes*) and white balls and a ballot box are provided for voting, where the question can be answered *yes* or *no*. The white ball answers *yes*, and the black one *no*. But other times the ballots are strips of paper upon which are printed, or written, *yes* or *no*, or the names of the candidates, as the case may be. These ballots are first distributed and are afterwards collected by tellers, either by being dropped into a hat or box by the brothers, who remain in their seats, or by the brothers coming to the ballot box and casting their ballot. The ballots should usually be folded when cast.

When everyone appears to have voted, the W. M. inquires if all have voted, and if so says, "The balloting is closed," (or words to that effect) whereupon the tellers proceed to count the ballots. If in unfolding the ballots it is found that two have been folded together, both are rejected as fraudulent. A blank piece of paper is not counted as a ballot and would not cause the rejection of the ballot with which it was folded. All blanks are ignored as simply wastepaper, and are not reported, the brothers who do not wish to vote adopting this method of concealing the fact. Small technical errors, like the misspelling of a word or name, should not be noticed if the meaning of the ballot is clear. For instance, where the name on the ballot sounds like the name of one of the candidates it should be so credited. If a ballot is written "Johnson," or "Johnston," or "Johnstone," it should be credited to the candidate whose name is one of these: but if there are two candidates with these names and no eligible brother with the name on the ballot, it must be rejected as illegal, or reported to the W. M., who will at once submit the question to the lodge as to whom the ballot should be credited. If these doubtful ballots will not affect the result, the tellers (many times the Secretary) may make their full report without asking for instructions in regard to them, placing these doubtful votes opposite the exact name as written on the ballot. Votes for ineligible persons and fraudulent votes should be reported under the heading of "Illegal Votes," after the legal votes. When two or three filled-out ballots are folded together they are counted as one fraudulent vote. The names of the candidates should be arranged in order, the one receiving the highest number of legal votes being first. In reporting the number of votes cast and the number necessary for election, all votes except blanks must be counted. Suppose the tellers find 100 ballot papers, 4 of which are blank. 1 contains two filled-out ones folded together, and 50 are cast for a person who is ineligible because of having held the office as long as permitted by the constitution: the tellers' report should be in this form:

Number of votes cast......................... 96
Necessary for election. 49
Br. A received 37
Br. B received................................. 8

Illegal Votes.

Br. C (ineligible) received 50
One ballot containing two for Br. D, folded
together, rejected as fraudulent 1

The teller first named, standing, addresses the W. M., reads the report and hands it to the W. M., and takes his seat, without saying who is elected. The W. M. again reads the report of the tellers and declares who is elected. In the case just given he says there is no election, stating the reason. If no one is elected, it is necessary to ballot again, and to continue balloting until there is an election. The W. M. should always vote in case of a ballot. When the tellers report, they should hand the ballots to the secretary, who should retain them until it is certain that the lodge will not order a recount which is within its power to do by a majority vote.

General Consent. Business can be expedited greatly by avoiding the formality of motions and voting in routine business and on questions of little importance, the W. M. assuming general (unanimous) consent until someone objects. It does not necessarily mean that every brother is in favor of the motion, but that knowing it is useless to oppose it, or even to discuss it, the opposition simply acquiesces in the informality. Thus, in the case of approving the minutes, the W. M. inquires if there are any corrections, and, if one is suggested, it is made: when no correction [or no further correction] is suggested, the W. M. says: "There being no corrections [or no further corrections] the minutes stand approved." While routine and minor matters can be rapidly disposed of in this way, if at any time objection is made with reasonable promptness, the W. M. ignores what has been done in that case even if he has announced the result, and requires a regular vote. [See also **48.**]

Proxy Voting, Absentee Voting & Voting by Mail. These forms of voting are not acceptable in a lodge setting and need not be discussed. Proxy voting *may* be acceptable in a Grand Lodge setting and the rules of such are explained by Grand Lodge law.

47. Votes that are Null and Void even if Unanimous.

No motion is in order that conflicts with the laws of the nation, or state, or Grand Lodge, or with the lodge's bylaws, and if such a motion is adopted, even by a unanimous vote, it is null and void.

48. Motions requiring more than a Majority Vote.

Majority Vote. Any legitimate motion not included among those mentioned below as requiring more than a majority vote, requires for its adoption only a majority; that is, more than half of the votes cast, ignoring blanks, at a legal meeting where a quorum is present, unless a larger vote for its adoption is required by the rules of the lodge.

General Consent or Unanimous Vote. By general, or unanimous, or silent, consent the lodge can do business with little regard for the rules of procedure, as they are made for the protection of the minority, and when there is no minority to protect, there is little use for the restraint of the rules, except such as protect the rights of absent brothers, or the right to a secret vote. In the former case the consent of the absentees cannot be given, and in the latter case the consent cannot be withheld by the minority without exposing their votes, which they cannot be compelled to do. One negative vote defeats a motion to make a vote unanimous, as a single objection defeats a request for general consent.

By the legitimate use of the principle that the rules are designed for the protection of the minority, and generally need not be strictly enforced when there is no minority to protect, business may be greatly expedited. When there is evidently no opposition, the formality of voting can be avoided by the W. M.'s asking if there is any objection to the proposed action, and if there is none, announcing the result. The action thus taken is said to be done by general consent, or unanimous or silent consent. Thus, after an order has been adopted limiting the speeches to two minutes each, if a speaker is so interesting that when his time has expired there is a general demand for him to go on, the W. M., instead of waiting for a motion and taking a vote, could accept it as the will of the lodge that the speaker's time be extended, and would direct him to proceed. Or, he might say that if there is no objection the brother's time will be extended two minutes, or some other time. [See also **46:16**]

Two-thirds Vote. A two-thirds vote means two-thirds of the votes cast, ignoring blanks which should never be counted. This must not be confused with a vote of two-thirds of the brothers present, or two-thirds of the brothers, terms sometimes used in bylaws. To illustrate the difference: Suppose 14 brothers vote on a question in a meeting of a lodge where 20 are present out of a total membership of 70, a two-thirds vote would be 10; a two-thirds vote of the brothers present would be 14; and a vote of two-thirds of the brothers would be 47.

There has been established as a compromise between the rights of the individual and the rights of the lodge the principle that a two-thirds vote is required to adopt any motion that suspends or modifies a rule of order previously adopted; or prevents the introduction of a question for consideration; or closes, or limits, or extends the limits of debate; or limits the freedom of nomination or voting; or closes nominations; or deprives one of membership or office. It will be found that every motion in the following list belongs to one of the classes just mentioned.

Motions Requiring a Two-thirds Vote.

Amend (Annul, Repeal, or Rescind) any part of the Constitution, Bylaws, or Rules of Order, previously adopted; it also requires previous notice- **66**

Art. IX

Committees and Boards

49. Committees Classified.

A Committee is a body of one or more members appointed or elected by a lodge to consider, or investigate, or act in regard to, certain matters or subjects, or to do all of these things. Committees may be divided into two distinct classes:

(1) Boards of Managers or Directors, Boards of Trustees, Executive Committees, etc.

(2) Ordinary Committees, Special or Standing, and Committee of the Whole and its substitutes.

These different kinds of committees are considered separately in the following five sections.

50. Boards of Managers, etc., and Executive Committees.

Committees of this class are essentially small deliberative groups, subordinate to the body that appoints them, with their duties and authority, and the number of their regular meetings and their quorums, defined by the parent body, or by its authority. The Executive Committee should be small, and the members should live near enough each other to be able to have frequent regular contacts, besides special meetings in emergencies. It is seldom that resolutions or other matters are referred to boards or committees of this class for them to report back to the lodge with recommendations. If papers are referred to them it is usually for their information and action. They are organized with a Chairman, who they elect if he is not appointed by the W.M. or bylaws of the lodge. Frequently the bylaws of the lodge make the W.M., ex-officio, [51] Chairman of such committees.

In a board meeting where there are not more than about a dozen present, for instance, it is not necessary to rise in order to make a motion, nor to wait for recognition by the Chairman before speaking or making a motion, nor for a motion to have a second; nor is there any limit to the number of speeches. The formalities necessary in order to transact business in a large lodge would hinder business in so small a body.

It is common for Boards to be composed of members who, with the consent of the W.M., remain in office for numerous years. The bylaws of some lodges also require that the members of certain committees be Past Masters or specific officers. Boards are sometimes constituted so that the term of office of, say, one-third of its members expire each year. All unfinished business falls to the ground when the new board is appointed.

It is customary for the bylaws to require an annual report from most committees, which usually gives a brief account of its doings for the year with recommendations for the future. After discussion, and amendment if necessary, the report is usually adopted by the lodge and recorded in the minutes as the report of the committee. In such a case, care should be taken in recording it to enclose in brackets all that has been struck out, and to put in italics whatever has been inserted, and to insert a note to that effect at the beginning of the report, so that exactly what the board recommended can readily be seen. The minutes should read thus: "The Board of Managers submitted its report which after discussion and amendment was adopted as follows, the words in brackets having been struck out and those underscored (in italics) having been inserted before the report was adopted." The lodge cannot alter the report of the board. It may decline to endorse it, or even to allow it to be recorded, but it cannot make it appear that the board stated anything different from what it has reported. By the above plan is shown exactly what the board reported and what the lodge adopted, or endorsed.

51. Ex-Officio Members of Boards and Committees.

Frequently boards and committees contain some members who are members by virtue of their office, and, therefore, are termed ex-officio members. When such a members ceases to hold the office his membership of the committee terminates automatically. There is no distinction between an ex-officio member and the other brother members except where the W.M. is ex-officio member (or Chairman) of all committees, in which case it is evidently the intention to permit, not to require, him to act as a member of the various committees, and therefore in counting a quorum he should not be counted as a member. The W.M. is not a member of any committee except by virtue of a special rule, or unless he is so appointed by the lodge.

52. Committees, Special and Standing.

It is usual in lodges, to have preliminary work in the preparation of matter for their action done by means of committees. The committee may be either a "standing committee," appointed for a definite time, as a meeting or a year; or a "special [or select] committee," appointed for a special purpose; or a "committee of the whole" consisting of the entire lodge. [For method of appointing committees of the whole, see **55**; other committees, see Commit, **32**.] Committees of the whole are not used much except in legislative bodies, and when the word committees is used in this Manual, unless specified to the contrary, standing or special committees are meant. Unless a chairman has been appointed, by either provisions in the bylaws or by the W.M., the first named on a committee becomes chairman, and should act as such unless the committee by a majority of its number elects a chairman, which it has the right to do if the lodge has not appointed one, and which a standing committee usually does. The Secretary should furnish him, or, in his absence, some other brother of the committee, with notice of the appointment of the committee, the names of the members, the papers or matter referred to it, and such instructions as the lodge has decided upon. Upon the committee's request, all papers and books necessary for the proper performance of its duties should be turned over to it by the proper officers.

It is the duty of the W. M. to call the committee together, but, if he neglects or declines to call a meeting of the committee, it is the duty of the committee to meet on the call of any two of its members. In small special committees the chairman usually acts as secretary, but in large ones and in all standing committees, it is customary to elect a secretary, who keeps a brief memorandum of what is done, for the use of the committee. Members of the lodge have a right to appear at the committee meetings and present their views on the subject before it at such reasonable times as, upon request, the committee may appoint. But during the deliberations of the committee no one has a right to be present, except the W.M. and members of the committee.

The rules of the lodge, as far as possible, apply to the committee, but motions to close or limit debate are not allowed, and there is no limit to the number of times a brother may speak, and unless the committee is very large, it is not necessary for anyone to rise and address the chairman before making a motion or speaking, nor does the chairman rise to put the question, nor are motions seconded. These formalities are unnecessary because the committee is so small, but, unless agreed to by general consent, all questions must be put to vote. Instead of the chairman's abstaining from speaking on questions, he is, usually, the most active participant in the discussions and work of the committee. In order that the lodge may have the benefit of the matured judgment of the committee, a reconsideration of a vote must be allowed regardless of the time and of previous reconsideration, and it may be moved by anyone who did not vote with the minority, even if he was absent when the previous vote was taken; but it shall require a two-thirds vote for its adoption unless every brother who voted with the majority is either present or received ample notice of the meeting and that the reconsideration was to be moved. This prevents taking advantage of the absence of members to reverse action, and enables brothers who were absent to bring up the question of reconsideration.

The committee constitutes a miniature lodge (of sorts), being able to act only when a quorum (a majority of the members) is present. If a paper is referred to them, they must not write on it, but should write their amendments on a separate sheet. If the amendments are numerous, it is better to write out a substitute and submit it. If a resolution is referred to a committee while a motion to postpone indefinitely is pending, only the resolution is referred to the committee, the motion to postpone indefinitely being ignored. If amendments are pending, they go to the committee, who may recommend their adoption or rejection, or make no recommendation in regard to them. If the committee originate the paper, all amendments must be incorporated in it. When they originate it, usually one brother has previously prepared a draft, which is read entirely through, and then read by paragraphs, the chairman pausing after each paragraph, and asking: "Are there any amendments proposed to this paragraph?" No vote is taken on the adoption of the separate paragraphs; but, after the whole paper has been read in this way, it is open to amendment generally, by striking out any paragraph, or by substituting or inserting new ones, or by substituting an entirely new paper for it. If there is a preamble it is considered last. When the entire paper has been amended to suit the committee, they should adopt it as their report, and request the W. M. or Secretary to report it to the lodge. When committees are appointed to investigate, or to report upon, certain matters, the report should close with, or be accompanied by, formal resolutions covering all recommendations, so that when their report is made no motion is necessary except to adopt the resolutions.

If the report is written in this form, "Your committee are of the opinion that Br. A's bill should be paid," there might be some doubt as to the effect of the adoption of the recommendation or the report. The report should close with a recommendation that the following order be adopted: "Ordered, That the treasurer pay Br. A's bill for $10.15." The committee should never leave to others the responsibility of preparing resolutions to carry out their recommendations. They should consider this as one of their most important duties.

When the report has been adopted by the committee a clear copy is made, usually commencing in a style similar to this: "The committee to whom was referred (state the matter referred), beg leave to submit the following report;" or, "Your committee appointed to (specify the object), respectfully report," etc. If the report is of much importance, it should be signed by all the members concurring in the report; but when it is of little importance, or merely recommends amendments, etc., it may be signed by the chairman alone, his signature being followed by the word "chairman." He should not, however, place "chairman" after his signature except when he signs the report alone and by the authority of the committee. The report must always be in the third person though written and signed by only one. The signature may be preceded by the words, "Respectfully and fraternally submitted," but it is not necessary.

Usually, the report is not dated or addressed, and sometimes it consists merely of a resolution, or a set of resolutions. In the latter case the chairman states he is instructed by the committee to submit and to move the adoption of the resolutions. The report of the majority is the report of the committee and should never be referred to as the majority report.

If the minority submit a report, (or more properly, their "views"), it may commence thus: "The undersigned, a minority of the committee appointed, etc., not agreeing with the majority, desire to express their views in the case." After the committee's report has been read and the motion to adopt has been made and the question stated, it is usual to allow the minority to present their views, but if anyone objects to its reception the W. M. should put the question to vote on its being received. It requires a majority vote to receive it, the question being undebatable. When the minority report is read it is for information, and it cannot be acted upon except by a motion to substitute it for the report of the committee. Whether the views of the minority are read or not, anyone can move to substitute the resolutions they recommend for those recommended by the committee. Where the minority cannot agree, each brother may submit his views separately. In some cases, a brother agrees to the report with a single exception, in which case instead of submitting his views separately, after all have signed who agree to the report, he may write that he agrees to the report except the part which he specifies, and then sign the statement.

The committee's report can contain only that which has been agreed to by a majority vote at a meeting of which every member has been notified, or at an adjourned meeting thereof (a quorum, a majority of the brothers, being present), except where it is impracticable to have a meeting of the committee, when it may contain what is agreed to by every brother.

A committee, except a committee of the whole, can appoint a subcommittee which, however, reports to the committee, and never to the lodge. This sub-committee must consist of members of the committee, except in cases where the committee is appointed to take action that requires the assistance of others, as to make arrangements for having a banquet. In such a case it is best to appoint the committee with power to appoint such subcommittees as are required; or, as is frequently done, to appoint the committee "with power," which means with power to take all the steps necessary to carry out its instructions. A committee has no power to punish its brothers for disorderly conduct, its recourse being to report the facts to the Worshipful Master. No allusion can be made in the lodge to what has occurred during the deliberations of the committee, unless it is by a report of the committee or by general consent. When a special committee is through with the business assigned it, a motion is made for the committee to "rise" (which is equivalent to the motion to adjourn without day), and that the chairman (or some brother who is more familiar with the subject) make its report to the lodge. A special committee ceases to exist as soon as the lodge receives its report. When a committee adjourns without appointing a time for the next meeting, it is considered as having adjourned at the call of the chairman, so that all the meetings of a special committee constitute one meeting. A meeting of a special committee may be called at any time by the chairman or by any two of its brothers, every brother being notified. When a committee adjourns to meet at another time, it is not necessary (though usually advisable) that absent brothers should be notified of the adjourned meeting.

A standing committee is either wholly, or partially, appointed at each annual election of lodge officers, and immediately thereafter it reorganizes by electing a chairman (unless he has been appointed by the W.M.) and a secretary (if necessary). Therefore, a standing committee must report at the annual election of officers meeting, or before, on everything referred to it during the year. The motion to rise is never used in standing committees or boards, nor is it used in other committees except when the committee is ready to report so that it will never meet again. A special committee is appointed for a specific purpose, and until the duty assigned it by the lodge is accomplished it continues to exist, unless sooner discharged, which requires a two-thirds vote if done without notice being given. When discharged, the chairman of the committee returns to the secretary all documents received from him.

While in small lodges, especially in those where but little business is done, there is not much need of many committees, in large lodges, or in those doing a great deal of business, committees are of the utmost importance. When a committee is properly selected, in nine cases out of ten its action decides that of the lodge. A committee for *action* should be small and consist only of those heartily in favor of the proposed action. If one not in sympathy with it is appointed, he should ask to be excused. A committee for deliberation or investigation of some matter (other than a candidate), on the contrary, should be larger, and represent all parties in the lodge, so that its opinion will carry with it as great weight as possible. The usefulness of the committee will be greatly impaired if any important faction of the lodge is unrepresented on the committee. The appointment of a committee is wholly explained in **32**.

53. Reception of reports.

When there is a place in the order of business provided for reports of committees, they are not made until they are called for by the Worshipful Master. Upon the arrival of the time for these reports, the W. M. calls for the reports of such officers and standing committees as are required to make reports, in the order in which they are arranged in the rules; after which he calls for the reports of the special committees in the order of their appointment. When called upon, the reporting member (who is the chairman of the committee, unless another brother is appointed to make the report) rises and addresses the W. M., and, when recognized, reads the report and hands it to the W.M., or the Secretary, and, when necessary, moves its adoption or acceptance as explained in the next section. If the committee reports back a paper with amendments, the amendments are read with sufficient of the related parts to make them understood.

If the order of business makes no provision for the report of the committee, the reporting brother, when ready to report, obtains the floor when no business is pending, and informs the W.M. that the committee to which was referred such a subject or paper has agreed upon a report which he is now prepared to submit. If the W. M. thinks the lodge wishes to hear the report, he directs him to proceed, whereupon he reads the report and hands it to the W. M. or Secretary and makes the proper motion for its disposal. If before it is read anyone objects to its reception, or if the W. M. is in doubt as to whether it should be received now, he may instruct the brother that the report will be read at another time.

If the report is a final one, when the lodge has received the report, the committee has completed its work, and, without any motion, it is automatically discharged from further consideration of the subject, and, if it is a special committee, it ceases to exist. If the report is only a partial one the committee is not discharged unless the lodge so votes or the W.M. so proclaims. If the subject is recommitted the committee is revived (unless the reference is to another committee), and all parts of the report that have not been adopted by the lodge are ignored by the committee as if the report had never been made. If any brother or brothers wish to submit the views of the minority it is customary to receive such a report immediately after receiving the report of the committee. In such case the reporting brother should notify the lodge that the views of the minority will be submitted in a separate paper. As soon as the W. M. has stated the question on the report, he should call for the views of the minority, which are then read for information. They cannot be acted upon unless it is moved to substitute them for the committee's report, or rather to substitute the recommendations of the minority for those of the committee.

A very common error is, after a report has been read, to move that it be received, whereas the fact that it has been read shows that it has been already received by the lodge. Another mistake, less common, but dangerous, is to vote that the report be accepted, which is equivalent to adopting it [see next section], when the intention is only to have the report up for consideration and afterwards to vote on its adoption.

54. Adoption or Acceptance of Reports.

When the report of a committee has been received, that is, has been presented to the lodge and either read or handed to the W. M. or the Secretary, the next business in order is the disposal of the report, the proper disposition depending upon its nature.

(1) If the report contains only a statement of fact or opinion for the information of the lodge, the reporting brother makes no motion for its disposal, as there is no necessity for action on the report. But if any action is taken, the proper motion, which should be made by someone else, is to "accept the report," which has the effect of endorsing the statement and making the lodge assume responsibility for it.

If it is a financial report, as in case of a treasurer, it should be referred to an auditing or finance committee, as the vote to accept the report does not endorse the accuracy of the figures, for the lodge can only be sure of that by having the report audited. Whenever such a financial report is made, the W. M., without any motion, should say it is referred to the finance committee or auditors, if there are any. If there are none, then the proper motion is to refer it to a finance committee to be appointed by the Worshipful Master. When the finance committee reports, this report should be accepted, or adopted, which carries with it the endorsement of the financial report.

(2) If the report contains recommendations not in the form of motions, they should all be placed at the end of the report, even if they have been given separately before, and the proper motion is to adopt the recommendations.

(3) If the report concludes with a resolution or a series of resolutions, the proper course is for the reporting brother to move that the resolution or resolutions be adopted or agreed to. This method should be adopted whenever practicable.

(4) If a committee reports back a resolution which was referred to it, the motion to postpone indefinitely, if it was pending, is ignored; if an amendment was pending it should be reported on. The form of the question to be stated by the W. M. depends upon the recommendation of the committee as follows:

(*a*) If the committee recommends its adoption, or makes no recommendation (where it can come to no agreement), the question should be stated on the amendment if there was one pending, and then on the resolution. These motions were pending when the question was referred to the committee, and therefore should not be made again.

(*b*) If the recommendation is that the resolution be not adopted, the question on the resolution, when it is put, should be stated thus: "The question is on the adoption of the resolution, the recommendation of the committee to the contrary notwithstanding." A similar course is pursued if the committee recommends that an amendment be not adopted.

(*c*) If the committee recommends that the resolution be postponed indefinitely, or postponed to a certain time, the question should be on the postponement, and, if that is lost, then on the resolution.

(*d*) If the committee reports back a resolution or paper with amendments, the reporting brother reads only the amendments with sufficient of the context to make them understood and then moves their adoption. The W. M., after stating the question on the adoption of the amendments, called for the reading of the first amendment, after which it is open for debate and amendment. A vote is then taken on adopting this amendment, and the next is read, and so on till the amendments are adopted or rejected, admitting amendments to the committee's amendments, but no others. When through with the committee's amendments, the W. M. pauses for any other amendments to be proposed by the members; and when these are voted on, he puts the question on agreeing to, or adopting, the paper as amended, unless, in a case like revising the bylaws, they have been already adopted. By suspending the rules [22], or by general consent, a report can be at once adopted without following any of the above routine.

If the amendments do not call for debate or amendment, as when reported from the committee of the whole, where they have been already discussed, the W. M. puts a single question on all the committee's amendments except those for which a brother asks a separate vote, thus "As many as are in favor of adopting the amendments recommended by the committee, except those for which a separate vote has been asked, say *aye*; those opposed say *no*."

He then takes up the remaining amendments separately in their order.

(*e*) If the committee reports back a resolution with a substitute which it recommends for adoption, the W. M. states the question on the substitute, if there were no amendments pending when the resolution was committed. If, however, amendments were pending when the resolution was committed, the W. M. first states the questions on those pending amendments, and when they are disposed of the states the question on the substitute. In either case the substitute is treated like any other substitute motion, the resolution being first perfected by amendments and then the substitute resolution. After both have been thus perfected the question is put on the substitution, and finally on the resolution. If the substitute is lost the resolution is open to amendments proposed by brothers.

(*f*) If the report is from the investigation committee of a candidate, the W. M. at once states the question on the reception of the candidate recommended by the committee.

A partial report of a committee is treated the same as the final report. If it reports progress only, without recommendations or conclusions, it is treated as any other report for information, and no action need be taken. But, if the partial report recommends action, then the question is to be put on adopting the report, or its recommendations, or the resolutions, the same as if it were the final report.

While it is customary to make and second a motion to accept or adopt a committee's report, yet if the motion is not made and the W. M. deems it best to have a vote taken on the question, he may state the appropriate question without waiting for a motion, accepting the submission of the report by a committee as equivalent to moving the adoption of the appropriate motion for disposing of it, just as is the case when one offers a resolution. To wait to see if two brothers are in favor of a proposition which at least two have signed, or authorized the W. M., or reporting brother, to sign, would appear useless.

When the W. M. has stated the question on the adoption of the recommendations or resolutions, or of the report, the matter under consideration is open to debate and amendment, and may have applied to it any of the subsidiary motions, like other main questions. Its consideration cannot be objected to if the matter was referred to the committee. While the report of the committee or its resolutions may be amended by the lodge, these amendments only affect that which the lodge adopts, as the lodge cannot in any way change the committee's report.

For example: A committee expresses the opinion that Br. A may have charged an excessive amount for an item sold to the lodge, and the lodge strikes out this statement from the report before adopting it. This does not alter the report, but, when the lodge adopts the report, this statement is not adopted. So, with a recommendation or a resolution: the lodge may strike out or add one or more recommendations or resolutions before adopting, but that does not alter the committee's report. If the proceedings are published, the committee's report should be printed exactly as it was submitted with the amendments printed below; or, still better, all words struck out should be enclosed in brackets and all words inserted should be printed in italics, and a note to that effect inserted at the beginning.

While the motions to adopt, to accept, etc., are often used indiscriminately, and the adoption of any one of them has the effect of endorsing or adopting the opinions, actions, recommendations, or resolutions submitted by the committee, as the case may be, yet it is better to use them as heretofore stated. If only one term is used, the word "adopt" is preferable, as it is least liable to be misunderstood.

55. Committee of the Whole.

In many jurisdictions, the considering of a question by a Committee of the Whole is out of order. In those jurisdictions which permit a Committee of the Whole, the following can be used.

When a lodge has to consider a subject which it does not wish to refer to a committee, and yet where the subject matter is not well digested and put into proper form for its definite action, or when, for any other reason, it is desirable for the lodge to consider a subject with all the freedom of an ordinary committee, it is the practice to refer the matter to the "Committee of the Whole." If it is desired to consider the question at once, the motion is made, "That the lodge do now resolve itself into a committee of the whole, to take under consideration," etc., or, "That we go into committee of the whole to consider," etc., specifying the subject. This is really a motion to "commit." [See **32** for its order of precedence, etc.] The committee is under the rules of the lodge, excepting as stated hereafter in this section.

The only motions in order are to amend and adopt, and that the committee "rise and report," as it cannot adjourn; nor can it order the "yeas and nays." Each brother can speak only once on the appeal. The only way to close or limit debate in committee of the whole is for the lodge, before going into committee of the whole, to vote that the debate in committee shall cease at a certain time, or that after a certain time no debate shall be allowed, excepting on new amendments, and then only one speech in favor of and one against it, of, say, five minutes each; or in some other way to regulate the time for debate.

If no limit is prescribed, any brother may speak as often as he can get the floor, and as long each time as is allowed in debate in the lodge, but he cannot speak a second time provided a brother wishes the floor who has not spoken on that particular question. Debate having been closed at a particular time by order of the lodge, the committee has not the power, even by unanimous consent, to extend the time. The committee cannot refer the subject to another committee. Like other committees, it cannot alter the text of any resolution referred to it; but if the resolution originated in the committee, then all the amendments are incorporated in it.

When the committee is through with the consideration of the subject referred to it, or if it wishes to adjourn, or to have the lodge limit debate, a motion is made that "the committee rise and report," etc., specifying the result of its proceedings. The motion to "rise" is always in order (except while voting or when another brother has the floor), and is undebatable and cannot be amended. As soon as this motion is adopted the W. M. addresses the lodge and says: "The Committee of the Whole has had under consideration (here he describes the resolution or other matter) and has directed me to report the same with (or without, as the case may be) amendments," provided the committee has concluded its business. If the committee has failed to come to a conclusion, strike out of the report all after "and has" and insert "come to no conclusion thereon." If no amendments are reported, the W. M. at once states the question on the resolution or other matter referred to the committee. If amendments are reported the reporting brother reads them, and hands the paper to the W. M., who reads, and states and puts the question on the amendments as a whole, unless a brother asks for a separate vote on one or more amendments, in which case a single vote is taken on all the other amendments, and then the question is stated separately on each of the amendments for which a separate vote was asked. The amendments may be debated and amended.

The Secretary does not record in the minutes the proceedings of the committee, but should keep a memorandum of the proceedings for its use.

In large lodges, where a brother can speak to any question only once, the committee of the whole seems almost a necessity, as it allows the freest discussion of a subject, while at any time it can rise and thus bring into force the strict rules of the lodge. In small lodges it is usually more convenient to substitute for it either the "Quasi (as if in) Committee of the Whole" or "Informal Consideration," as frequently used in ordinary societies. These are explained in the next two sections.

56. As if in Committee of the Whole

As if in (or Quasi) Committee of the Whole is more convenient in small lodges. The motion should be made in a form similar to this: "I move that the resolution be considered as if in committee of the whole." This being adopted, the question is open to debate and amendment with all the freedom of the committee of the whole. If any motion is adopted, except an amendment, it puts an end to the quasi committee of the whole. Thus, the motion to commit is equivalent to the following motions when in committee of the whole: (1) That the committee rise; (2) that the committee of the whole be discharged from the further consideration of the subject; and (3) that it be referred to a committee. When the lodge has finished amending the proposition under consideration, without further motion the W.

M. announces that, "The lodge, acting as if in committee of the whole, has had such subject under consideration, and has made certain amendments," which he then reports. The subject comes before the lodge then as if reported by a committee, the W. M. stating the question on the amendments as described at the close of the previous section under committee of the whole. The secretary should keep a memorandum of the proceedings while acting as if in committee of the whole, but it should not be entered in the minutes, being only for temporary use. The W. M.'s report to the lodge should be entered in the minutes, as it belongs to the lodge's proceedings.

57. Informal Consideration.

In lodges where the meetings are not large, instead of going into committee of the whole, or considering questions as if in committee of the whole, it is more usual to consider the question informally. The motion is made thus: "I move that the question be considered informally." The effect of the adoption of this motion is to open the main question and any amendments that may be proposed, to free debate as if in committee of the whole. No brother can speak the second time to the same question as long as a brother who has not spoken desires the floor. This informal consideration applies only to the main question and its amendments, so that any other motion that is made is under the regular rules of debate. While considering a question informally the lodge by a two-thirds vote may limit the number or length of speeches, or in any other way limit or close the debate. While the consideration of the main question and its amendments is informal, all votes are formal, the informality applying only to the number of speeches allowed in debate. The instant the main question is disposed of temporarily, or permanently, the informal consideration automatically ceases without any motion or vote.

If the question is considered in either the regular committee of the whole or the quasi committee of the whole, it is necessary formally to report the action to the lodge and then act on the report. Thus, it will be seen that informal consideration is much simpler than either of the methods described in the previous two sections. It can be used to advantage in lodges that are not very large, instead of the committee of the whole. While this is not a motion to commit, yet it is used for practically the same purpose as the committee of the whole. It ranks just below the motion "to consider as if in committee of the whole," which is just below "to go into committee of the whole."

Art. X

The Officers and the Minutes

58. Worshipful Master
59. Secretary
60. The Minutes
61. Treasurer

58. Worshipful Master.

The presiding officer of a Masonic lodge is the Worshipful Master. In debate, he is referred to by his official title and is addressed by prefixing "Worshipful Brother" to his name. In referring to himself (or someone else who has held this position), he should never use the personal name; he generally says, "the Worshipful Master," which means the presiding officer of the lodge, whoever may hold that office.

His parliamentary duties are generally as follows: To set the craft to labor at the time at which the lodge is to meet, calling the brothers to order; to announce the business before the lodge in the order in which it is to be acted upon [63]; to recognize brothers entitled to the floor [3]; to state [6] and to put to vote [9] all questions which are regularly moved, or necessarily arise in the course of the proceedings, and to announce the result of the vote; to protect the lodge from annoyance from evidently frivolous or dilatory motions by refusing to recognize them [40]; to assist in the expediting of business in every way compatible with the rights of the brothers, as by allowing brief remarks when undebatable motions are pending, if he thinks it advisable; to restrain the brothers when engaged in debate, to enforce on all occasions the observance of order and decorum among the brothers, deciding all questions of order; to inform the lodge, when necessary, or when referred to for the purpose, on a point of order or practice pertinent to pending business; to authenticate, by his signature, when necessary, all the acts, orders, and proceedings of the lodge declaring its will and in all things obeying its commands.

During debate, he should be seated and pay attention to the speaker, who is required to address his remarks to the East. He should always refer to himself as "the Worshipful Master," thus, "The Worshipful Master decides," etc., not "I decide," etc. When a brother has the floor, the W. M. should not interrupt him except as provided in [3], so long as he does not transgress any of the rules of the lodge.

He is entitled to vote when the vote is by ballot (but not after the tellers have commenced counting the ballots) and in all other cases where the vote would change the result. Thus, in a case where a two-thirds vote is necessary, and his vote thrown with the minority would prevent the adoption of the question, he can cast his vote; so, also, he can vote with the minority when it will produce a tie vote and thus cause the motion to fail; but he cannot vote twice, first to make a tie, and then to give the casting vote. The W. M. should not hesitate to put the question on a motion to appoint delegates or a committee on account of his being included.

The W. M. should not permit the object of a meeting to be defeated by a few factious persons using parliamentary forms with the evident object of obstructing business. In such a case, he should refuse to entertain the dilatory or frivolous motion. But the W. M. should never adopt such a course merely to expedite business when the opposition is not factious. It is only justifiable when it is perfectly clear that the opposition is trying to obstruct business. [See Dilatory Motions, **40**].

In the absence of the W. M., the Senior Warden normally assumes the duties of the Master. In the absence of the S.W., the Junior Warden accepts the duties. In the absence of all three principal officers, most lodges cannot open.

The W. M. should not only be familiar with parliamentary usage and set the example of strict conformity thereto, but he should be a man of executive ability, capable of controlling men. He should set an example of courtesy and should never forget that to control others, it is necessary to control one's self. A nervous, excited W. M. can scarcely fail to cause trouble in a meeting. No rules will take the place of tact and common sense on the part of the Master. While usually he need not wait for motions of routine, or for a motion to be seconded when he knows it is favored by others, yet if this is objected to, it is safer instantly to require the forms of parliamentary law to be observed. By general consent, many things can be done that will save much time [see **48**], but where the lodge is very large or is divided and contains members who are habitually raising points of order, the most expeditious and safe course is to enforce strictly all the rules and forms of parliamentary law. He should be especially careful after every motion is made, and every vote is taken to announce the next business in order. Whenever an improper motion is made, instead of simply ruling it out of order, it is well for the W. M. to suggest how the desired object can be accomplished. [See "Hints to Inexperienced Worshipful Masters" below.]

The bylaws sometimes state that the W.M. shall appoint all committees. In such cases, the lodge may authorize committees, but cannot appoint or nominate them. Some bylaws make the W.M. an ex-officio member of every committee. Where this is done, he has the rights of other members of the committees, but not the obligation to attend every committee meeting. [See **51**.]

A W. M. will often find himself perplexed by difficulties attending his position. In such cases, he will do well to remember that parliamentary law was made for lodges, and not the lodges for parliamentary law. This is well expressed by a distinguished English writer on parliamentary law, thus: "*The great purpose of all rules and forms is to subserve the will of the body rather than to restrain it; to facilitate, and not to obstruct, the expression of their deliberative sense.*"

Additional Duties of the Master and the Wardens.

In addition to his duties as presiding officer, in many lodges the W.M. has duties as an administrative or executive officer. Where this is desired, the bylaws should clearly set forth these duties, as they are outside of his duties as presiding officer of the lodge and do not come within the scope of parliamentary law.

The same thought is true of Wardens. It must not be forgotten that in the case of the absence of the W. M., the Senior Warden must often preside, and in case of the illness, or resignation, or death of the W. M. that the Senior Warden becomes acting W.M. for the unexpired term unless the bylaws or Grand Lodge specify how vacancies shall be filled. It is a mistake to elect a Warden who is not competent to perform the duties of a Master.

Hints to Inexperienced Worshipful Masters.

While in the East, keep your lodge and Grand Lodge Constitution, Bylaws, and Rules of Order next to you, which should be studied until you are perfectly familiar with them. You cannot tell the moment you may need this knowledge. If a brother asks what motion to make in order to attain a certain object, you should be able to tell him at once. **[10.]** You should memorize the list of ordinary motions arranged in their order of precedence so quickly that there will be no delay in deciding all points contained in it. Become familiar with the first ten sections of these Rules; they are simple and will enable you to master parliamentary law quickly. Carefully read the various sections so as to become accustomed to the ordinary methods of conducting business in lodges. Notice that there are different ways of doing the same thing, all of which are allowable.

You should know all the business to regularly come before the meeting and call for it in its regular order. Have with you a list of members of all committees to guide you in nominating new committees.

When a motion is made, do not recognize any brother or allow anyone to speak until the motion is seconded and you have stated the question; or, in case of there being no second and no response to your call for a second, until you have announced that fact; except in case of a main motion before it is seconded or stated someone rises and says he rises to move a reconsideration, or to call up the motion to reconsider, or to move to take a question from the table. In any of these cases, you should recognize the interrupting brother as entitled to the floor [3]. If you have made a mistake and assigned the floor to the wrong person or recognized a motion that was not in order, correct the error as soon as your attention is called to it. So, when a vote is taken, announce the result and also what question, if any, is then pending before recognizing any brother that addresses the WM. Never wait for mere routine motions to be seconded when you know no one objects to them. [See **8**.]

If a brother makes an improper motion, do not quickly rule it out of order but courteously suggest the proper one. If it is moved "to lay the question on the table until 8 P.M.," as the motion is improper, ask if the intention is "to postpone the question to 8 P.M.;" if the answer is yes, then state that the question is on the postponement to that time. If it is moved simply "to postpone the question," without stating the time, do not rule it out of order, but ask the mover if he wishes "to postpone the question indefinitely" (which kills it) or "to lay it on the table" (which enables it to be taken up at any other time); then state the question in accordance with the motion he intended to make. So, if after a report has been presented and read, a brother moves that "it be received," ask him if he means to move "its adoption" (or "acceptance," which is the same thing) as the report has been already received. No vote should be taken on receiving a report, which merely brings it before the lodge, and allows it to be read, unless someone objects to its reception.

The chairman of a committee usually has the most to say in reference to questions before the committee. Still, the W. M. of a lodge, especially a large one, should, of all the brothers, have the least to say upon the merits of pending questions.

Never interrupt brothers while speaking simply because you know more about the matter than they do; never get excited; never be unjust to the most troublesome brother, or take advantage of his ignorance of parliamentary law, even though a temporary good is accomplished thereby.

Know parliamentary law, but do not try to show off your knowledge. Never be technical or stricter than is absolutely necessary for the good of the meeting. Use your judgment; the lodge may be of such a nature through its ignorance of parliamentary usages and peaceable disposition that strict enforcement of the rules would greatly hinder business instead of assisting. But in large lodges, where there is much work to be done, and especially where there is a liability to trouble, the only safe course is to require strict observance of the rules.

59. Secretary.

The officer in a Masonic Lodge charged with recording all proper to be written is called the Secretary. The Secretary is the recording officer of the lodge and the custodian of its records, except those specifically assigned to others, as the treasurer's books. These records are open, however, to inspection by any brother at reasonable times. Where a committee needs any records of the lodge for the proper performance of its duties, they should be turned over to its chairman. The same principle applies in boards and committees, their records being accessible to brothers of the board or committee, as the case may be, but to no others.

In addition to keeping the records of the lodge and the minutes of the meetings, it is the duty of the secretary to keep a register, or roll, of the brothers and to call the roll when required; to notify officers, committees, and delegates of their appointment, and to furnish committees with all papers referred to them and delegates with credentials; and to sign with the W.M. all orders on the treasurer authorized by the lodge, unless otherwise specified in the bylaws. He should also keep one book in which the constitution, bylaws, rules of order, and standing rules should all be written, leaving every other page blank. Whenever an amendment is made to any of them, in addition to being recorded in the minutes, it should be immediately entered on the page opposite to the article amended, with a reference, in red ink, to the date and page of the minutes where it is recorded.

In addition to the above duties, it is his duty to send out proper notices of all called meetings and other meetings when necessary and to conduct the correspondence of the lodge, except as otherwise provided.

The secretary can, before each meeting, for the use of the W. M., make out an order of business [63], showing in their exact order what is necessary to come before the lodge. He should also have, at each meeting, a list of all standing committees and such special committees as are in existence at the time, as well as the bylaws of the organization and its minutes. He should keep a record of the proceedings, stating what was done and not what was said, unless it is to be published, and never making criticisms, favorable or otherwise, on anything said or done. This record, usually called the minutes, is kept as explained in the next section. When a committee is appointed, the secretary should hand the names of the committee and all papers referred to it, to the W. M., or some other of its members. He should indorse on the reports of committees the date of their reception, and what further action was taken upon them, and preserve them among the records for which he is responsible. It is not necessary to vote that a report be "placed on file," as that should be done without a vote, except in organizations that habitually keep no records except their minutes and papers ordered on file.

60. The Minutes.

The record of the proceedings of a lodge is usually called the Minutes. The essentials of the record are as follows: (a) the kind of meeting, "regular" (or stated) or "special" ; (b) name of the lodge; (c) date of meeting and place, when it is not always the same; (d) the fact of the presence of the W. M. and Secretary, or in their absence the names of their substitutes, (e) whether the minutes of the previous meeting were approved, or their reading dispensed with, the dates of the meetings being given when it is customary to occasionally transact business at other than the regular business meetings; (f) all the main motions (except such as were withdrawn) and points of order and appeals, whether sustained or lost, and all other motions that were not lost or withdrawn; (g) and usually the hours of meeting and adjournment, when the meeting is solely for business. Generally, the name of the brother who introduced a main motion is recorded, but not of the seconder.

In some lodges, the minutes are signed by the W.M. in addition to the secretary, and when published, they should always be signed by both officers. If minutes are not habitually approved at the next meeting, then there should be written at the end of the minutes the word "Approved" and the date of the approval, which should be signed by the secretary. They should be entered in good black ink in a well-bound record book. In some lodges, the Secretary enters the minutes by use of computers. In such cases, a printed copy of the minutes should be made to ensure a permanent record.

The *Form* of the *Minutes* may be as follows:

> At a regular (or special) meeting of M. L. Lodge #123, held in their hall, on Thursday evening, March 19, 2005, the following officers were present: [name all officers present]. The minutes of the previous meeting were read and approved. The Committee on Relief reported the names of Bros. C and D as being in need and rendered such assistance as possible. The committee on .... reported through Br. G a series of resolutions, which were thoroughly discussed and amended, and finally adopted, as follows:

Resolved,

That...............................

The lodge was closed in due and ancient form at 10 P.M.

John Doe, P.M.

Secretary

In keeping the minutes, much depends upon the kind of meeting and whether the minutes are to be published (most lodges do NOT publish their minutes). In the meetings of lodges, there is no object in reporting the details of debates; the duty of the secretary, in such cases, is mainly to record what is "done" by the lodge and not what is said by the brothers. He should enter the essentials of a record, as previously stated, and when a count has been ordered or where the vote is by ballot, he should enter the number of votes on each side; and when the voting is by yeas and nays, he should enter the result of the vote. The proceedings of the committee of the whole, or while acting as if in committee of the whole, should not be entered in the minutes, but the report of the committee should be entered. When a question is considered informally, the proceedings should be kept as usual, as the only informality is in the debate. If a report containing resolutions has been agreed to, the resolutions should be entered in full as finally adopted by the lodge, thus: "The committee on .... submitted a report with a series of resolutions which, after discussion and amendment, were adopted as follows:" then should be entered the resolutions as adopted. Where the proceedings are published, the method shown further on should be followed. If the report is of great importance, the lodge should order it "to be entered on the minutes," in which case the secretary copies it in full upon the record.

Where the regular meetings are held weekly, bi-monthly, or monthly, the minutes are read at the opening of each meeting and, after correction, should be approved. When the reading of the minutes is dispensed with, they can afterward be taken up at any time when nothing is pending. If not taken up previously, they come before the lodge at the next meeting before the reading of the last minutes. With this exception the motion to dispense with reading the minutes is practically identical to the motion to lay the minutes on the table, being undebatable and requiring only a majority vote.

Minutes to be Published. When the minutes are to be published, in addition to the strict record of what is done, as previously described, they should contain a list of the speakers on each side of every question, with an abstract of all addresses, if not the addresses in full, when written copies are furnished. Reports of committees should be printed exactly as submitted, the minutes showing what action was taken by the lodge in regard to them, or they may be printed with all additions in italics and parts struck out enclosed in brackets, in which case a note to that effect should precede the report or resolutions. In this way, the reader can see exactly what the committee reported and also exactly what the lodge adopted or endorsed.

61. Treasurer.

This officer, in the majority of cases, acts as a banker, merely holding the funds deposited with him and paying them out on the order of the lodge signed by the W.M. and the Secretary. He is always required to make an annual report, and in many lodges, he also makes a quarterly report which may be in the form given on the next page. If the lodge has auditors, the report should be handed to them, with the vouchers, in time to be audited before the meeting. The auditors, having certified its correctness, submit their report, and the W. M. puts the question on adopting it, which has the effect of approving the treasurer's report and relieving him from responsibility in case of loss of vouchers, except in case of fraud. If there are no auditors, the report, when made, should be referred to a finance committee, which should report on it later.

It should always be remembered that the financial report is made for the information of the membership. The details of dates and separate payments for the same object are a hindrance to its being understood. They are useless, as it is the duty of the auditing committee to examine into details and see if the report is correct. The following brief report is in a form adapted to many lodges where the financial work is a very subordinate part of their work:

REPORT OF THE TREASURER OF M. L. LODGE #123
FOR THE QUARTER ENDING MARCH 31, 2005.

Receipts.

Balance on hand January 1, 2005	$ 825.75
Initiation fees	$150.00
Dues Collected	$850.00
Donations	$210.50
Total	$2035.75

Disbursements.

Rent of Hall	$ 980.00
Electric lights	$322.00
Stationery and Printing	$75.00
Repair of Furniture	$110.00
Tiler	$160.00

Total	$1647.00

Balance on hand March 31, 2005
Total .... $ 388.75

S........ M........,
Treasurer

Examined and found correct.

R........ V........ }
J........ L........ }
Auditing Committee.

Art. XI

Miscellaneous

62. Quorum

A quorum of a lodge is such a number as must be present so that business can be legally transacted. The quorum refers to the number present, not to the number voting. In a lodge of Master Masons, the quorum is normally seven members, of which the W.M. or a Warden must be present. The quorum for a lodge of Entered Apprentice or Fellowcraft Masons may be less than seven members. Still, if the lodge bylaws or Grand Lodge law states that business of the lodge can only be transacted in the Master Masons degree, no business can take place if less than seven members are present.

63. Order of Business.

It is customary for every lodge to adopt an order of business for its meetings. When no rule has been adopted, the order in **Appendix A** can be used.

The minutes are read only once a meeting at the beginning of the meeting. The order includes the reports of all Boards or Committees and reports of such officers as required to make them. The order also includes, first, the business pending and undisposed of at the close of the previous meeting; then the general orders that were on the calendar for the previous meeting and were not disposed of; and finally, matters postponed to this meeting that have not been disposed of.

At every meeting, the Secretary should always have a memorandum of the order of business for the use of the W.M., showing everything to come before the lodge. The W. M., as soon as one thing is disposed of, should announce the next business in order. When reports are in order, he should call for the different reports in their order. When unfinished business is in order, he should announce the different questions in their proper order, as stated above, and thus always keep control of the business.

If it is desired to transact business out of its order, it is necessary to suspend the rules [22], which can be done at the will of the Worshipful Master. But, as each resolution or report comes up, a majority can at once lay it on the table and thus reach any question it desires first to dispose of. It is improper to lay on the table or to postpone a class of questions like reports of committees or, in fact, anything but the question before the lodge.

64. Nominations and Elections.

Before proceeding to an election to fill an office, it is customary to nominate one or more candidates. This nomination is unnecessary when the election is by ballot or roll call, as each brother may vote for any eligible person, whether nominated or not. When the vote is viva voce or by rising, the nomination is like a motion to fill a blank, the different names being repeated by the W. M. as they are made, and then the vote is taken on each in the order in which they were nominated until one is elected. The nomination need not be seconded. Sometimes a nominating ballot is taken to ascertain the preferences of the brothers. But in the election of the officers of a lodge, it is more usual to have the nominations made by a committee (if it is done at all). When the committee makes its report, which consists of a ticket, the W. M. asks if there are any other nominations, when they may be made from the floor. The committee's nominations are treated as if made by brothers from the floor, with no vote being taken on accepting them. When the nominations are completed, the lodge proceeds to the election, the voting being by any of the methods mentioned under Voting [**46**], unless the bylaws prescribe a method. The usual method in lodges is by ballot. The balloting continues until all offices are filled. In some lodges, the W.M. and Wardens vote seated with the ballot box brought to their stations. It is customary for all members of the lodge to be required to place a ballot in the ballot box. An election takes effect immediately if the candidate is present and does not decline or if he is absent and has consented to his candidacy. If he is absent and has not consented to his candidacy, it takes effect when he is notified of his election, provided he does not decline immediately. After the election has taken effect and the officer or brother has learned the fact, it is too late to reconsider the vote on the election. An officer-elect officially takes possession of his office once he is installed, unless the rules specify the time. In most lodges, the time of installation must be clearly designated.

65. Constitutions, Bylaws, Rules of Order, and Standing Rules.

The rules of a lodge, in most cases, may be conveniently divided into these four classes, though in some lodges, all the rules are found under one of these heads, being called either the constitution, the bylaws, or the standing rules.

Such provisions in regard to the constitution, etc., as are of a temporary nature should not be placed in the constitution, etc., but should be included in the motion to adopt, thus: "I move the adoption of the constitution reported by the committee and that the four directors receiving the most votes shall serve for three years, the four receiving the next largest numbers shall serve for two years, and the next four for one year, and that where there is a tie the classification shall be by lot;" or, "I move the adoption, etc....... and that Article III, shall not go into effect until after the close of this annual meeting." Or, if the motion to adopt has been made, it may be amended so as to accomplish the desired object.

Constitutions. An incorporated lodge (there are many) sometimes has no constitution, the state charter of incorporation taking its place, and many others prefer to combine under one head the rules that are more commonly placed under the separate heads of constitution and bylaws. Some lodges use the Grand Lodge constitution and laws with little additional laws of the lodge. When the bylaws are elaborate, it is better to separate and place the most important rules in the constitution. The constitution should contain only the following:

(1) Name and object of the lodge.
(2) Jurisdiction of the lodge.
(3) Officers and their election.
(4) Meetings of the lodge (including only what
is essential, leaving details to the bylaws).
(5) How to amend the constitution.

These can be arranged into five articles, or the first one may be divided into two, in which case there would be six articles. Usually, some of the articles should be divided into sections. Nothing should be placed in the constitution that may be suspended, except in the case of requiring elections of officers to be by ballot, in which case the requirement may be qualified so as to allow the ballot to be dispensed with by a unanimous vote when there is but one candidate for the office. The constitution should require previous notice of an amendment and also a two-thirds or three-fourths vote for its adoption. [See Amendments to Constitutions, etc., **66.**]

Bylaws should include all the rules that are of such importance that they cannot be changed in any way without previous notice, except those placed in the constitution and the rules of order. Few lodges adopt any special rules of order of their own under that name, contenting themselves with putting a few such rules in their bylaws and then being bound by Grand Lodge law and adopting some standard work on parliamentary law as their authority. When a lodge is incorporated, the state charter of incorporation may take the place of the constitution. In such a case, the bylaws would contain all the rules of the lodge, except those in the charter that cannot be changed without previous notice. The bylaws should always provide for their amendment, as shown in **66.** It should be expressly provided for if it is desired to permit the suspension of any bylaw. Bylaws, except those relating to business procedure, cannot be suspended unless they expressly provide for their suspension. Bylaws in the nature of rules of order may be suspended by a two-thirds vote, as stated in **22.**

The parliamentary and non-esoteric duties of the W.M. and the Secretary of a lodge are defined in **58** and **59**. But in all lodges, other duties are required of these officers, and these, together with the duties of the other officers, are defined in Masonic tradition and law. If a lodge wishes to provide for honorary officers or members, it is well to do so in the bylaws. Unless the bylaws state the contrary, these positions are simply complimentary, carrying with them the right to attend the meetings and to speak but not to make motions or to vote. Honorary Past Masters, or Past Wardens should sit in places of honor, if so provided, but they do not, by virtue of their honorary office, preside over the lodge. An honorary office is not strictly an office and in no way conflicts with a brother's holding a real office or being assigned any duty. It is the same as if he did not hold the honorary office. Like a university honorary degree, it is perpetual unless rescinded. So, it is proper, where desired, to include in the published list of honorary officers the names of all upon whom the honor has been conferred, even though deceased.

Rules of Order should contain only the rules relating to the orderly transaction of business in the meetings and to the parliamentary duties of the officers. There is no reason why most of these rules should not be the same for all lodges, and there is a great advantage in uniformity of parliamentary procedure, as far as possible. Lodges should, therefore, adopt some generally accepted rules of order as their parliamentary authority and then adopt only such special rules of order as are needed to supplement that authority. Every lodge, in its bylaws, should adopt a rule like this: "The rules contained in [specifying the work on parliamentary practice] shall govern the lodge in all cases to which they are applicable, and in which they are not inconsistent with the bylaws of this lodge and laws of the Grand Lodge of ...." Without such a rule, anyone so disposed can cause great trouble in a meeting.

Standing Rules should contain only such rules as may be adopted without previous notice by a majority vote at any business meeting. The vote on their adoption, or their amendment, before or after adoption, may be reconsidered. At any meeting, they may be suspended by a majority vote or amended or rescinded by a two-thirds vote. If notice of the proposed action was given at a previous meeting or in the call for this meeting, it may be amended or rescinded by a majority vote. As a majority may suspend any of them for that meeting, these rules do not interfere with the freedom of any meeting and therefore require no notice in order to adopt them. Generally, they are not adopted at the organization of a lodge, but from time to time, as they are needed. Sometimes the bylaws of a lodge are called standing rules, but it is better to follow the usual classification of rules as given in this section. The following is an example of a standing rule:

Resolved, That the meetings of this lodge from April 1 to September 30 shall begin at 7:30 P.M., and during the rest of the year at 8 P.M.

No standing rule, resolution, or motion is in order that conflicts with the constitution, bylaws, rules of order, or standing rules.

66. Amendments of Constitutions, Bylaws, and Rules of Order.

Constitutions, bylaws, and rules of order, which have been adopted and contain no rule for their amendment, may be amended at any regular business meeting. If the amendment was submitted in writing at the previous regular business meeting, then it may be amended by a two-thirds vote of those present. But each lodge should adopt rules for the amendment of its constitution, bylaws, and rules of order, adapted to its own case, but always requiring previous notice and a two-thirds vote. The requirements should vary to suit each lodge's needs, always providing ample notice to the membership. In specifying when the amendment must be submitted, "the previous regular meeting" should be used instead of "a previous regular meeting," as in the latter case, action on the amendment might be delayed indefinitely to suit the mover and the object of giving notice be defeated. In prescribing the vote necessary for the adoption of an amendment, the expression "a vote of two-thirds of the members" should never be used, as it is seldom that two-thirds of the members — that is, two-thirds of the entire membership — is ever present at a meeting. If it is desired to require a larger vote than two-thirds (that is, two-thirds of the votes cast), the expression "a vote of two-thirds of the members present" should be used. Instead of submitting the amendment in writing, sometimes only notice, or written notice, of an amendment is required. Unless the notice is required to be in writing, it may be given orally. In any case, only the purport of the amendment is necessary, unless the rule requires that the amendment itself shall be submitted.

Unless lodge of Grand Lodge rules differ, if a committee is appointed to revise the bylaws and report at a certain meeting, this would be all the required notice. The amendments could be immediately acted upon if the bylaws required only previous notice of an amendment. But if they required the amendment, or "notice of such amendment," to be submitted at the previous regular meeting, the revision could not be taken up until the next regular meeting after the committee had submitted its report. The committee may submit a substitute for the bylaws unless it is limited as to its report, as a substitute is an amendment. Great care should be exercised in amending constitutions, etc., to comply with every rule in regard to their amendment.

An amendment to the constitution, or anything else that has already been adopted, goes into effect immediately upon its adoption unless the motion to adopt specifies a time for its going into effect, or the lodge has previously adopted a motion to that effect. While the amendment is pending, a motion may be made to amend by adding a proviso similar to this, "Provided that this does not go into effect until after the close of the final meeting in December." Or, while the amendment is pending, an incidental motion may be adopted that, in case the amendment is adopted, it shall not take effect until a specified time. This requires only a majority vote.

Amending a proposed amendment to the constitution, etc., may be accomplished by a majority vote, without notice, subject to certain restrictions. The lodge is not limited to adopting or rejecting the amendment just as it is proposed. Still, no amendment is in order that increases the modification of the rule to be amended, as otherwise advantage could be taken of this by submitting a very slight change that would not attract attention and then moving the serious modification as an amendment to the amendment.

Thus, if the bylaws placed the annual dues at $50.00, and an amendment is pending to strike out 50 and insert 75, an amendment would be in order to change the 50 to any number between 50 and 75; but an amendment would not be in order that changed the 75 to any number greater than 75 or less than 50. Had notice been given that it was proposed to increase the dues to more than 75 dollars or to reduce them below 50 dollars, members might have been present to oppose the change who did not attend because they were not opposed to an increase as high as 75 dollars. The same principle applies to an amendment in the nature of a substitute, the proposed substitute being open to amendments that diminish the changes, but not to amendments that increase those that are proposed or introduce new changes. Thus, if an amendment is pending, substituting a new rule for one that prescribes the initiation fee and annual dues, and the substitute does not change the annual dues, then a motion to amend it so as to change the annual dues would be out of order. The notice must be sufficiently definite to give fair warning to all parties interested regarding the exact points to be modified. The proposed amendment is a main motion, and that is the only question before the lodge. It is subject to amendments of the first and second degree, like other main motions, and no amendment that is not pertinent to it is in order.

A lodge can amend its bylaws so as to affect any supplemental duties of officers already elected (such as the Junior Warden supplying refreshments for meetings). If it is desired that the amendment should not affect officers already elected, a motion to that effect should be adopted before voting on the amendment, or the motion to amend could have added to it the proviso that it should not affect officers already elected. There is something in the nature of a contract between a lodge and its officers which either one can modify to some extent, or even terminate. Still, it must be done with reasonable consideration for the other party. The Secretary, for instance, has no right to refuse to perform his duties on the grounds that he has handed in his resignation. On the other hand, the lodge cannot compel him to continue in office beyond a reasonable time to allow for choosing his successor.

Care should be exercised in wording the sections providing for amending the constitution, etc., to avoid such tautology as "amend, or add to, or repeal," or "alter or amend," or "amend or in any way change." The one-word *amend*ment covers any change in the constitution, etc., whether it is a word or a paragraph that is added or struck out, replaced by another word or paragraph, or whether a new constitution, etc., is substituted for the old one.

Art. XII.

Organization and Meetings.

67. Regular Meeting of a lodge
68. Online Lodge Meetings

67. Regular Meetings of a Lodge.

After a lodge is properly organized, its regular business meetings are conducted as follows: When the hour fixed for the meeting to begin arrives, the W. M. calls the meeting to order and directs the secretary to read the minutes of the last meeting. When they are read, he asks, "Are there any corrections to the minutes?" If none are suggested, he adds, "There being none, the minutes stand approved as read." If any corrections are suggested, the secretary makes them unless there is opposition. If there is a difference of opinion, someone moves to amend the minutes, or the W. M., without waiting for a motion, may put the question on the amendment that has been suggested. When this has been settled, the W. M. asks, "Are there any further corrections (or amendments) to the minutes?" If there is no response, he adds, "There being none, the minutes stand approved as corrected." He then announces the next business in order, following the order of business prescribed by the rules of the lodge.

If the order of business is the same as given in **Appendix A**, as soon as the reception and reference of new petitions is finished, the W. M. says, "The next business in order is hearing the reports of the standing committees." He may then call upon each committee in its order for a report, thus: "Has the committee on charity any report to make?" In this case, the committee may report as shown above, or some member of it may reply that it has no report to make. Or, when the W. M. knows that there are but few, if any, reports to be made, it is better, after making the announcement of the business, for him to ask, "Have these committees any reports to make?" After a short pause, if no one rises to report, he states, "There being no reports from the standing committees, the next business in order is hearing the reports of special committees," when he will act the same as in the case of the standing committees. The W. M. should always have a list of the committees to enable him to call upon them, as well as to guide him in the appointment of new committees.

Having attended to the reports of committees, the W. M. announces the next business in order, and so on, until the business of the meeting has been disposed of, and the lodge can be closed.

The meetings of different lodges can vary greatly, and they should be managed differently in order to obtain the best results. Some lodges require strict enforcement of parliamentary rules, while with others the best results will be obtained by being more informal. It is important that the W.M. have tact and common sense, especially with a lodge composed of many past masters.

68. Online Lodge Meetings

The COVID-19 pandemic of 2020 prevented many lodges, often by state law, from holding meetings or gathering in groups. Even after restrictions were lifted, many lodges were required by their Grand Lodge to modify how meetings and gatherings were held. The technology for online gatherings existed prior to 2020, but many lodges did not show much interest in this new method of assembly. With the restrictions resulting from the pandemic, lodges began to find value in online gatherings, even if only to virtually visit with members of the lodge.

But while these gatherings are beneficial for wellness checks, educational presentations, and simple online business duties, they can be challenging for actual lodge meetings. Several points must be considered.

1. No online meeting or venue can be considered a tyled (tiled) meeting. All online gatherings must be considered public events. Hacking any online venue is not difficult for anyone with computer skills. Treat everything said and done online as if it was going into the local public newspaper or shown on the local television station. "Online" equals "public."

2. Organization and planning are vital for any sort of online lodge gathering. In an actual lodge setting, everyone except, maybe, new Masons know how they should act, where they sit, and how a lodge meeting operates. Online lodge gatherings are, for most, completely new settings. Participants may be sitting in their living room or den in front of their computer. The lodge *feel* is nonexistent. It is easy for chaos to develop. The W.M. needs to quickly and clearly explain the rules under which the gathering

will be conducted. The W.M. should not assume that members know what can or cannot be done in such online meetings.

3. As explained elsewhere in this book, all aspects of meeting procedure should be followed except where the question enters into any area of the esoteric, not permitted to be written, or private aspects of a meeting.

See **58** and **59** for all nonesoteric aspects of online lodge gatherings or meetings concerning the duties of the W.M. or Secretary. See also **67** for regular practices of lodge meetings.

If the W.M. is not experienced in the operation of the online venue that the lodge chooses to utilize, one experienced in the operation of the venue should serve as the host of the meeting and control all operations. The W.M. should, in advance of the meeting, inform the host of what he wants to happen during the meeting. A rehearsal should be held with the W.M., host, any necessary participants, and officers at least one day before the meeting to ensure that all is working and all grasp the operation and plans.

If Grand Lodge permission needs to be secured prior to holding any online activities by your lodge, this must be done prior to the gathering and in accordance with the policies of your Grand Lodge. Allow enough time to receive permission before you hold your event. Contact your Grand Secretary's office before the event if anything is unclear.

Do not deviate from the intended reason for the gathering. If you are calling a meeting for the purpose of an educational lecture, then conduct no business at such an event. The W.M. should begin the event by introducing his officers and acknowledging any Grand Lodge Officers who may be present. The speaker should then be introduced and given the "floor." A speaker should be considered as a "necessary participant" and be included in any rehearsal. If images or graphics are used in the lecture, then they should be tested at the rehearsal to make sure that the operation is smooth and with no unexpected problems. If a Q&A session is desired, then you should preplan how the questions will be submitted and limit the Q&A session to no longer than the talk itself. The host should attempt to screen questions to avoid silly or nonrelevant questions. The key is to preplan and rehearse so as to avoid as many unexpected problems as possible.

Your Grand Lodge will decide how much, if any, business you are allowed to conduct online. Your lodge bylaws and Grand Lodge rules and regulations will determine procedures that must be followed. For example: if a Ballot Box is required in your by-laws or Grand Lodge for any question, then anything requiring the use of a Ballot Box cannot be resolved online without permission from your Grand Lodge. If you have any questions about whether an action is permissible, contact your Grand Secretary's office.

Lodge decorum should be maintained even in online settings. The host of an online gathering (if not the W.M.) should maintain strict control over the ability of members to speak. Permission to speak should be made to the W.M. by raising a hand or by whatever means the venue allows. The W.M. should allow any and all to speak on relevant matters. However, the W.M. always reserves the right to suspend discussions at his pleasure.

Online gathers can augment lodge meetings as a novel and cost-effective means to bring speakers to the lodge who live at great distances from the lodge. The speaker can speak from his home, and the lodge members can all benefit from such lectures from their homes or in the lodge itself with a screen and computer. By taking advantage of advancing technologies, a lodge can find creative ways to improve the entire lodge experience.

A lodge can use online gatherings to grow or renew interest in lodge activities by maintaining order and following simple rules.

Art. XIII

Legal Rights of Lodges and Trial of Their Members

69. Right of a Lodge to Punish its Members
70. Trial of Members of Lodges

69. The Right of a Lodge to Punish its Members.

A lodge has the inherent right to make and enforce its own laws and punish an offender, the extreme penalty, however, being expulsion from its own body. When expelled, the lodge has the right, for its own protection, to give public notice that the person has ceased to be a member of that lodge. But it has no right to go beyond what is necessary for self-protection and publish the charges against the brother. In a case where a member of an organization was expelled, and an officer of the organization published, by its order, a statement of the grave charges upon which he had been found guilty, the expelled member recovered damages from the officer in a suit for libel, the court holding that the truth of the charges did not affect the case.

70. Trial of Members of Lodges.

Every lodge, having the right to purify its own body, must therefore have the right to investigate the character of its members and punish those found guilty of offenses. Charges made against members of the lodge must be investigated by the means proscribed by Grand Lodge law. If the charges call for Masonic trial, then the procedure for Masonic trial as laid out by the Grand Lodge must be followed. As the procedures for trial can vary greatly from jurisdiction to jurisdiction, no attempt will be made in this work to establish a set form for Masonic trial.

Appendix

Appendix A

ORDER OF BUSINESS

Below is a suggested Order of Business. The Worshipful Master may change the following to suit his convenience.

A. Opening the Lodge.
B. Reading of the minutes of the last stated and/or called communications. (Minutes may be read aloud or provided in printed form for later review, depending on the rules or laws of the jurisdictions.)
C. Reading and acting on correspondence.
D. Reports of investigating committees.
E. Balloting on petitions and applications.
F. Reception and reference of new petitions for the degrees and applications for membership, restoration and advancement.
G. Reports of standing committees:
    (1) On Charity.
    (2) On Finance and Budget.
    (3) On Masonic Education.
    (4) On Other Matters.
H. Reports of special committees.
I. Unfinished business.
J. New business.
K. Degree work, including examination of candidates.
L. Remarks for the Good of the Order.
M. Closing the Lodge.

Appendix B

PREROGATIVES OF THE WORSHIPFUL MASTER

1. To congregate his Lodge upon any emergency.
2. To preside at all communications of his Lodge
3. To fill temporarily all vacancies that may occur in the Lodge offices, unless otherwise provided by the constitution and by-laws.
4. To regulate the admission of visitors.
5. To control and terminate discussions.
6. To be the custodian and preserve the Charter of the Lodge, and transmit it to his successor.
7. To determine all questions of Order and of Business.
8. To appoint all committees.
9. To order the issuance of notifications to members.
10. To give the casting vote in case of a tie, in addition to his own vote. This is limited, however, to votes taken by voice or by upraised hands.
11. To sign all drafts upon the Treasurer for the payment of Lodge disbursements, by order of the Lodge. Nor may the Treasurer lawfully pay out the funds without such order.
12. To represent the Lodge in Grand Lodge.
13. To appoint the Senior Deacon and such other officers as may be prescribed in the bylaws of the Lodge.
14. To install his successor.
15. To refuse to initiate a candidate, notwithstanding his acceptance by the Lodge, if in his judgment, such initiation would be improper.
16. To order a second ballot when the first is unfavorable taking care that the necessary precautions be observed.
17. To discuss all questions without regard to the parliamentary etiquette of leaving the chair, because it is his duty at all times to give the Craft guard and wholesome instruction.
18. To be exempt from trial by his Lodge. The Grand Lodge alone has penal jurisdiction over him.

Appendix C

THE 25 ANCIENT LANDMARKS OF FREEMASONRY
by Albert Mackey

Editor's Note:

This collection of "Landmarks" is presented as a tool for Masonic education. It should not be confused with the actual law of any particular Grand Lodge. Grand Lodges are the bodies that establish, define, and publish lists of landmarks that are accepted by their jurisdiction. The landmarks of one jurisdiction do not always agree with the landmarks of other jurisdictions.

The most famous collection of landmarks is the 25 landmarks offered below by Brother Albert Mackey. They are offered as the 25 Landmarks that were in the opinion of Bro. Mackey most significant to Freemasons.

For the landmarks that are approved and accepted by your Grand Lodge, it is advised that you contact your Grand Lodge office.

— MRP

LANDMARK FIRST
The modes of RECOGNITION are, of all the Landmarks, the most legitimate and unquestioned. They admit of no variation; and if ever they have suffered alteration or addition, the evil of such a violation of the ancient law has always made itself subsequently manifest. An admission of this is to be found in the proceedings of the Masonic Congress at Paris, where a proposition was presented to render these modes of recognition once more universal — a proposition which never would have been necessary, if the integrity of this important Landmark had been rigorously preserved.

LANDMARK SECOND
THE DIVISION OF SYMBOLIC MASONRY INTO THREE DEGREES is a Landmark that has been better preserved than almost any other, although even here the mischievous spirit of innovation had left its traces, and by the disruption of its concluding portion from the Third Degree, a want of uniformity has been created in respect to the final teaching of the Master's order, and the Royal Arch of England, Scotland, Ireland, and America, and the "high degrees" of France and Germany, are all made to differ in the mode in which they lead the neophyte to the great consummation of all symbolic masonry.

In 1813, the Grand Lodge of England vindicated the ancient Landmark, by solemnly enacting that ancient craft Masonry consisted of the three degrees: Entered Apprentice, Fellow Craft, and Master Mason, including the Holy Royal Arch; but the disruption has never been healed, and the Landmark, although acknowledged in its integrity by all, still continues to be violated.

LANDMARK THIRD

The Legend of the THIRD DEGREE is an important Landmark, the integrity of which has been well preserved. There is no rite of Masonry, practiced in any country or language, in which the essential elements of this legend are not taught. The lectures may vary, and indeed are constantly changing, but the legend has ever remained substantially the same; and it is necessary that it should be so, for the legend of the Temple Builder constitutes the very essence and identity of Masonry; any rite which should exclude it, or materially alter it, would at once, by that exclusion or alteration, cease to be a Masonic rite.

LANDMARK FOURTH

THE GOVERNMENT OF THE FRATERNITY BY A PRESIDING OFFICER called a Grand Master, who is elected from the body of the craft, is a Fourth Landmark of the Order. Many persons ignorantly suppose that the election of the Grand Master is held in consequence of a law or regulation of the Grand Lodge. Such, however, is not the case. The office is indebted for its existence to a Landmark of the Order. Grand Masters are to be found in the records of the institution long before Grand Lodges were established; and if the present system of legislative government by Grand Lodges were to be abolished, a Grand Master would be necessary. In fact, although there has been a period within the records of history, and indeed of very recent date, when a Grand Lodge was unknown, there never has been a time when the craft did not have their Grand Master.

LANDMARK FIFTH

The prerogative of the Grand Master to preside over every assembly of the craft, wheresoever and whensoever held, is a fifth Landmark. It is in consequence of this law, derived from ancient usage, and not from any special enactment, that the Grand Master assumes the chair, or as it is called in England, "the throne," at every communication of the Grand Lodge; and that he is also entitled to preside at the communication of every Subordinate Lodge, where he may happen to be present.

LANDMARK SIXTH

The prerogative of the Grand Master to grant Dispensations for conferring degrees at irregular times, is another and a very important Landmark. The statutory law of Masonry requires a month, or other determinate period, to elapse between the presentation of a petition and the election of a candidate. But the Grand Master has the power to set aside or dispense with this probation, and allow a candidate to be initiated at once. This prerogative he possessed in common with all Masters, before the enactment of the law requiring a probation, and as no statute can impair his prerogative, he still retains the power, although the Masters of Lodges no longer possess it.

LANDMARK SEVENTH

The prerogative of the Grand Master to give dispensations for opening and holding Lodges is another Landmark. He may grant, in virtue of this, to a sufficient number of Masons, the privilege of meeting together and conferring degrees. The Lodges thus established are called "Lodges under Dispensation." They are strictly creatures of the Grand Master, created by his authority, existing only during his will and pleasure, and liable at any moment to be dissolved at his command. They may he continued for a day, a month, or six months; but whatever be the period of their existence, they are indebted for that existence solely to the grace of the Grand Master.

LANDMARK EIGHTH

The prerogative of the Grand Master to make masons at sight, is a Landmark which is closely connected with the preceding one. There has been much misapprehension in relation to this Landmark, which misapprehension has sometimes led to a denial of its existence in jurisdictions where the Grand Master was perhaps at the very time substantially exercising the prerogative, without the slightest remark or opposition. It is not to be supposed that the Grand Master can retire with a profane into a private room, and there, without assistance, confer the degrees of Freemasonry upon him. No such prerogative exists, and yet many believe that this is the so much talked of right of "making Masons at sight." The real mode and the only mode of exercising the prerogative is this: The Grand Master summons to his assistance not less than six other masons, convenes a Lodge, and without any previous probation, but on sight of the candidate, confers the degrees upon him, after which he dissolves the Lodge and dismisses the brethren. Lodges thus convened for special purposes are called occasional lodges," This is the only way in which any Grand Master within the records of the institution has ever been known to "make a Mason at sight." The prerogative is dependent upon that of granting dispensations to open and hold Lodges. If the Grand Master has the power of granting to any other Mason the privilege of presiding over Lodges working by his dispensation, he may assume this privilege of presiding to himself; and as no one can deny his right to revoke his dispensation granted to a number of brethren at a distance, and to dissolve the Lodge at his pleasure, it will scarcely be contended that he may not revoke his dispensation for a Lodge over which he himself has been presiding, within a day, and dissolve the Lodge as soon as the business for which he had assembled it is accomplished. The making of Masons at sight is only the conferring of the degrees by the Grand Master, at once, in an occasional Lodge, constituted by his dispensing power for the purpose, and over which he presides in person.

LANDMARK NINTH

The necessity of masons to congregate in lodges is another Landmark. It is not to be understood by this that any ancient Landmark has directed that permanent organization of subordinate Lodges which constitutes one of the features of the Masonic system as it now prevails, but the landmarks of the Order always prescribed that Masons should from time to time congregate together, for the purpose of either operative or speculative labor, and that these congregations should be called Lodges. Formerly these were extemporary meetings called together for special purposes, and then dissolved, the brethren departing to meet again at other times and other places, according to the necessity of circumstances. But warrants of constitution, bylaws, permanent officers and annual arrears, are modern innovations wholly outside of the Landmarks, and dependent entirely on the special enactments of a comparatively recent period.

LANDMARK TENTH

The government of the craft, when so congregated in a Lodge by a Master and two Wardens, is also a Landmark. To show the influence of this ancient law, it may be observed by the way, that a congregation of Masons meeting together under any other government, as that for instance of a president and vice-president, or a chairman and sub chairman, would not be recognized as a Lodge. The presence of a Master and two Wardens is as essential to the valid organization of a Lodge as a warrant of constitution is at the present day. The names, of course, vary in different languages, the Master, for instance, being called "Venerable" in French Masonry, and the Wardens "Surveillants," but the officers, their number, prerogatives and duties, are everywhere identical.

LANDMARK ELEVENTH

The necessity that every lodge, when congregated, should be duly tiled, is an important Landmark of the institution, which is never neglected. The necessity of this law arises from the esoteric character of Masonry. As a secret institution, its portals must of course be guarded from the intrusion of the profane, and such a law must therefore always have been in force from the very beginning of the Order. It is therefore properly classed among the most ancient Landmarks. The office of Tiler is wholly independent of any special enactment of Grand or Subordinate Lodges, although these may and do prescribe for him additional duties, which vary in different jurisdictions. But the duty of guarding the door, and keeping off cowans and eavesdroppers, is an ancient one, which constitutes a Landmark for the government.

LANDMARK TWELFTH

The right of every mason to be represented in all general meetings of the craft and to instruct his representatives, is a twelfth Landmark. Formerly, these general meetings, which were usually held once a year, were called "General Assemblies," and all the fraternity, even to the youngest Entered Apprentice, were permitted to be present. Now they are called "Grand Lodges," and only the Masters and Wardens of the Subordinate Lodges are summoned. But this is simply as the representatives of their members. Originally, each Mason represented himself; now he is represented by his officers. This was a concession granted by the fraternity about 1717, and of course does not affect the integrity of the Landmark, for the principle of representation is still preserved. The concession was only made for purposes of convenience.

LANDMARK THIRTEEN

The Right of every mason to appeal from the decision of his brethren in Lodge convened, to the Grand Lodge or General Assembly of Masons, is a Landmark highly essential to the preservation of justice, and the prevention of oppression. A few modern Grand Lodges, in adopting a regulation that the decision of Subordinate Lodges, in cases of expulsion, cannot be wholly set aside upon an appeal, have violated this unquestioned Landmark, as well as the principles of just government.

LANDMARK FOURTEENTH

THE RIGHT OF EVERY MASON TO VISIT and sit in every regular Lodge is an unquestionable Landmark of the Order. This is called "the right of visitation." This right of visitation has always been recognized as an inherent right, which insures to every Mason as he travels through the world. And this is because Lodges are justly considered as only divisions for convenience of the universal Masonic family. This right may, of course be impaired or forfeited on special occasions by various circumstances; but when admission is refused to a Mason in good standing, who knocks at the door of a Lodge as a visitor, it is to be expected that some good and sufficient reason shall be furnished for this violation, of what is in general a Masonic right, founded on the Landmarks of the Order.

LANDMARK FIFTEENTH

It is a Landmark of the Order that no visitor, unknown to the brethren present, or to some one of them as a Mason, can enter a Lodge without first passing an examination according to ancient usage. Of course, if the visitor is known to any brother present to be a Mason in good standing, and if that brother will vouch for his qualifications, the examination may be dispensed with, as the Landmark refers only to the cases of strangers, who are not to be recognized unless after strict trial, due examination, or lawful information.

LANDMARK SIXTEENTH

No Lodge can interfere in the business of another Lodge, nor give degrees to brethren who are members of other Lodges, This is undoubtedly an ancient Landmark, founded on the great principles of courtesy and fraternal kindness, which are at the very foundation of our institution. It has been repeatedly recognized by subsequent statutory enactments of all Grand Lodges.

LANDMARK SEVENTEENTH

It is a Landmark that every freemason is Amenable to the Laws and Regulations of the masonic jurisdiction in which he resides, and this although he may not be a member of any Lodge. Non-affiliation, which is, in fact a Masonic offense, does not exempt a Mason from Masonic Jurisdiction.

LANDMARK EIGHTEENTH

Certain qualifications of candidates for initiation are derived from a Landmark of the Order. These qualifications are that he shall be a man, shall be unmutilated, free born, and of mature age. That is to say, a woman, a cripple, or a slave, or one born in slavery, is disqualified for initiation into the rites of Masonry. Statutes, it is true, have from time to time been enacted, enforcing or explaining these principles; but the qualifications really arise from the very nature of the Masonic institution, and from its symbolic teachings, and have always existed as landmarks.

LANDMARK NINETEENTH

A belief in the existence of God as the GRAND ARCHITECT of the universe, is one of the most important Landmarks of the Order. It has been always deemed essential that a denial of the existence of a Supreme and Superintending Power, is an absolute disqualification for initiation. The annals of the Order never yet have furnished or could furnish an instance in which an avowed atheist was ever made a Mason. The very Initiatory ceremonies of the first degree forbid and prevent the possibility of so monstrous an occurrence.

LANDMARK TWENTIETH

Subsidiary to this belief in God, as a Landmark of the Order, is the belief in a resurrection to a future life. This Landmark is not so positively impressed on the candidate by exact words as the preceding; but the doctrine is taught by very plain implication and runs through the whole symbolism of the Order. To believe in Masonry, and not to believe in a resurrection, would be an absurd anomaly, which could only be excused by the reflection, that he who thus confounded his belief and his skepticism, was so ignorant of the meaning of both theories as to have no rational foundation for his knowledge of either.

LANDMARK TWENTY-FIRST

It is a Landmark, that a "Book of the Law" shall constitute an indispensable part of the furniture of every Lodge. I say advisedly, a Book of the Law, because it is not absolutely required that everywhere the Old and New Testaments shall be used. The "Book of the Law" is that volume which, by the religion of the country, is believed to contain the revealed will of the Grand Architect of the universe. Hence, in all Lodges in Christian countries, the Book of the Law is composed of the Old and New Testaments; in a country where Judaism was the prevailing faith, the Old Testament alone would be sufficient; and in Mohammedan countries, and among Mohammedan Masons the Koran might be substituted. Masonry does not attempt to interfere with the peculiar religious faith of its disciples, except as far as relates to the belief in the existence of God, and what necessarily results from that belief." The Book of the Law is to the speculative Mason his spiritual Trestle- board; without this he cannot labor; whatever he believes to be the revealed will of the Grand Architect constitutes for him this spiritual Trestleboard, and must ever be before him in his hours of speculative labor, to be the rule and guide of his conduct. The Landmark, therefore, requires that a Book of the Law, a religious code of some kind, purporting to be an exemplar of the revealed will of God, shall form in essential part of the furniture of every Lodge.

LANDMARK TWENTY-SECOND

THE EQUALITY OF ALL MASONS is another Landmark of the Order. This equality has no reference to any subversion of those gradations of rank which have been instituted by the usages of society. The monarch, the nobleman or the gentleman is entitled to all the influence and receives all the respect which rightly belong to his exalted position. But the doctrine of Masonic equality implies that, as children of one great Father, we meet in the Lodge upon the level—that on that level we are all traveling to one predestined goal, that in the Lodge genuine merit shall receive more respect than boundless wealth, and that virtue and knowledge alone should be the basis of all Masonic honors, and be rewarded with preferment When the labors of the Lodge are over, and the brethren have retired from their peaceful retreat, to mingle once more with the world, each will then again resume that social position, and exercise the privileges of that rank, to which the customs of society entitle him.

LANDMARK TWENTY-THIRD

The secrecy of the institution is another and a most important Landmark. There is some difficulty in precisely defining what is meant by a "secret society." If the term refers, as perhaps in strictly logical language it should, to those associations whose designs are concealed from the public eye, and whose members are unknowing which produce their results in darkness, and whose operations are carefully hidden from the public gaze — a definition which will be appropriate to many political clubs and revolutionary combinations in despotic countries, where reform, if it is at all to be effected, must be effected by stealth—then clearly Freemasonry is not a secret society. Its design is not only publicly proclaimed, but is vaunted by its disciples as something to be venerated; its disciples are known, for its membership is considered an honor to be coveted; it works for a result of which it boasts, the civilization, and reformation of his manners. But if by a Secret society is meant, and this is the most popular understanding of the term, a society in which there is a certain amount of knowledge, whether it be of methods of recognition, or of legendary and traditional learning, which is imported to those only who have passed through an established form of initiation, the form itself being also concealed or esoteric, then in this sense is Freemasonry undoubtedly a secret society. Now this form of secrecy is a form inherent in it, existing with It from its very foundation, and secured to it by its ancient Landmarks. If divested of its secret character, it would lose its identity, and would cease to be Freemasonry. Whatever objections may, therefore, be made to the institution, on account of its secrecy, and however much some unskillful brethren have been willing in times of trial, for the sake of expediency, to divest it of its secret character, it will be ever impossible to do so, even were die Landmark not standing before us as an insurmountable obstacle; because such change of its character would be social suicide, and the death of the Order would follow its legalized exposure. Freemasonry, as a secret association, has lived unchanged for centuries an open society it would not last for as many years.

LANDMARK TWENTY-FOURTH

The foundation of a Speculative Science upon an Operative Art, and the symbolic use and explanation of the terms of that art, for purposes of religious or moral teaching, constitute another Landmark of the Order. The Temple of Solomon was the cradle of the institution," and, therefore, the reference to the operative Masonry, which constructed that magnificent edifice, to the materials and implements which were employed in its construction, and to the artists who were engaged in the building, are all component and essential parts of the body of Freemasonry, which could not be subtracted from it without an entire destruction of the whole identity of the Order. Hence, all the comparatively modern rites of Masonry, however they may differ in other respects, religiously preserve this temple history and these operative elements, as the substratum of all their modifications of the Masonic system.

LANDMARK TWENTY-FIFTH

The last and crowning Landmark of all is, that these Landmarks can never be changed. Nothing can be subtracted from them — nothing can be added to them — not the slightest modification can be made in them. As they were received from our predecessors, we are bound by the most solemn obligations of duty to transmit them to our successors. Not one jot or one title of these unwritten laws can be repealed; for in respect to them, we are not only willing but compelled to adopt the language of the sturdy old barons of England —*"Nolumus legen mutari."*

Appendix D

THE LANDMARKS
From
Masonic Jurisprudence
By Roscoe Pound

By landmarks in Freemasonry, we are generally supposed to mean certain universal, unalterable and unrepealable fundamentals which have existed from time immemorial and are so thoroughly a part of Masonry that no Masonic authority may derogate from them or do aught but maintain them. Using constitution in the American political sense, they may be said to be the prescriptive constitution of Freemasonry.

Not long ago it was a general article of Masonic belief that there were such landmarks. The charge to the Master Mason taken by our American monitors from Preston's *Illustrations*, seemed to say so. The first and second charges to the master in the installation service (numbered 10 and 11 in Webb's version) — also taken from Preston's *Illustrations* — seemed to say so. The books on Masonic jurisprudence in ordinary use and Masonic cyclopedias told us not only that there were landmarks but exactly what the landmarks were in great detail. Probably any master of an American lodge of a generation ago, who was reasonably well posted, would have acquiesced in the confident dogmatism of Kipling's Junior Deacon, who "knowed the ancient landmarks" and "kep' 'em to a hair." Hence it may well shock many even now, to tell them that it is by no means certain that there are any landmarks at all—at least in the sense above defined.

For myself, I think there are such landmarks. But I must confess the question is not so clear as to go without argument in view of the case which has been made to the contrary.

Accordingly, I conceive that there are two questions which the student of Masonic jurisprudence must investigate and determine: (1) Are there landmarks at all; (2) if so, what are the landmarks of the Craft? And in this investigation, as I conceive, he will find his path made straighter if he attends carefully to the distinction between the landmarks and the common law of Masonry, which I attempted to explain in my former lecture.

It is well to approach the question whether there are landmarks historically. The first use of the term appears to have been in Payne's *General Regulations*, published with *Anderson's Constitutions of 1723*. Payne was the second Grand Master after the revival of 1717. If entirely authentic, these regulations, coming from one who took a prominent part in the revival would be entitled to the very highest weight. But many believe that

Anderson took some liberties with them, and if he did, of course to that extent the weight of the evidence is impaired. There is no proof of such interpolation or tampering — only a suspicion of it.

Hence in accord with what seem to me valid principles of criticism, I must decline to follow those who will never accept a statement of Anderson's, credible in itself, without some corroboration, and shall accept Anderson's *Constitutions* on this point at their face value.

How then does Payne (or Anderson) use the term "landmark"? He says: "The Grand Lodge may make or alter regulations, provided the old landmarks be carefully preserved." It must be confessed this is not clear. Nearly all who have commented on the use of the term in Payne's Regulations, as reported by Anderson, have succeeded in so interpreting the text as to sustain their own views. Perhaps there could be no better proof that the text is thoroughly ambiguous. Three views as to what is meant seem to have support from the text.

One view is that Payne used the word landmark in the sense in which we now commonly understand it. This is consistent with the text and has in its favor the uniform belief of Masons of the last generation, the Prestonian charge to the Master Mason and the Prestonian installation ceremony. I should have added tradition, were I sure that the tradition could be shown to antedate the end of the eighteenth century, or indeed to be more than a result of the writings of Dr. Mackey, in combination with the charges just referred to. A second view is that Payne used the word landmark in the sense of the old traditional secrets of the operative Craft and hence that for use today the term can mean no more than a fundamental idea of secrecy. This interpretation is urged very plausibly by Bro. Hextall, P. Prov. G. M. of Derbyshire, in an excellent paper on the landmarks — entitled The Old Landmarks of the Craft — in the *Transactions of Quatuor Coronati Lodge*, vol. 25, p. 91.

A third view is that Anderson, finding the term in Payne's *Regulations*, where the word was used in an operative sense — for Payne undoubtedly used operative manuscripts — used it without inquiry into its exact meaning, and without troubling himself as to how far it had a concrete meaning, and so made it available as a convenient and euphonious term to which others might attach a meaning subsequently as Masonic law developed. This last view, which eminent authorities now urge, is a fair specimen of the uncharitable manner in which it is fashionable among Masonic scholars to treat the father of Masonic history. But it should be said that such a phenomenon would have an exact counterpart in the law of the land under which we live. Historians are now telling us of the "myth of Magna Charta," and it is undoubtedly true that the immemorial rights and privileges of Englishmen which our fathers asserted at the Revolution were at least chiefly the work of Sir Edward Coke in the seventeenth century and that he succeeded in finding warrant therefor in what we have since regarded as the charters of civil liberty. Nevertheless, Coke was right in finding in these charters the basis for a fundamental scheme of individual rights. And may we not say that Mackey was equally right in insisting upon a scheme of Masonic jural fundamentals and finding warrant therefor in his books in the references to the landmarks, even if Payne and Anderson were not very clear what they meant? Next, we may inquire how the term has been used since Anderson's Constitutions.

In 1775 Preston, in his *Illustrations of Masonry*, clearly uses the word landmarks as synonymous with established usages and customs of the Craft — in other words as meaning what I have called Masonic common law. This is indicated by the context in several places. But it is shown conclusively by two passages in which he expressly brackets "ancient landmarks" with "established usages and customs of the order" as being synonymous. He does this in referring to the ritual of the Master Mason's degree, which in each case he says preserves these ancient landmarks. Preston's *Illustrations of Masonry* was expressly sanctioned by the Grand Lodge of England. Hence, we have eighteenth- century warrant for contending that everything which is enjoined in the Master Mason's obligation is a landmark. But, if this means landmark in the sense of merely an established custom, we are no better off. Perhaps one might argue that the Grand Lodge of England was more concerned with sanctioning the proposition that the Master's degree preserved ancient landmarks than with Preston's definition of a landmark! However, this may be, it is manifest that here, as in the case of Anderson, there is very little basis for satisfactory argument.

Some further light is thrown on Preston's views by the charge to the Master Mason and the charges propounded to the Master at installation, as set forth in the *Illustrations of Masonry*. The former may well refer to the landmarks contained in the Master Mason's obligation. The proposition in the latter, however, suggests the idea of an unalterable prescriptive fundamental law. The Master-elect is required to promise to "strictly conform to every edict of the Grand Lodge or General Assembly of Masons that is not subversive of the principles and groundwork of Masonry." Also, he is required to testify "that it is not in the power of any man or body of men to make alterations or innovations in the body of Masonry." These principles, this groundwork, this body of Masonry, whether we use the term landmarks or not, convey the very idea which has become familiar to us by that name.

The next mention of landmarks is in Ashe's Masonic Manual, published in 1813. But Ashe simply copies from Preston.

In 1819 the Duke of Suffolk, G. M. of England, issued a circular in which he said: "It was his opinion that so long as the Master of the lodge observed exactly the landmarks of the Craft, he was at liberty to give the lectures in the language best suited to the character of the lodge over which he presided." The context here indicates clearly that he simply meant the authorized ritual.

Next, we find the term used by Dr. George Oliver in a sermon before the Provincial Grand Lodge of Lincolnshire in 1820. In this sermon Oliver tells us that our "ancient landmarks" have been handed down by oral tradition. But he does not suggest what they are nor does he tell us the nature of a landmark. Afterwards in 1846 Oliver published his well-known work in two large volumes entitled *Historical Landmarks of Freemasonry*.

One will look in vain to this book, however, for any suggestion of Dr. Oliver's views on the matter we are now discussing. The book is an account of the history of the Craft, and the word landmark in the title is obviously used only in the figurative sense of important occurrences — as the phrase "beacon light," for example, is used in Lord's *Beacon Lights of History*. Oliver does not use the term again till his Symbol of Glory, in 1850. In that book he asks the question: "What are the landmarks of Masonry, and to what do they refer"—in other words, the very thing we are now discussing. His answer is most disappointing. He begins by telling us that what landmarks are and what are landmarks "has never been clearly defined." He then explains that in his book, Historical Landmarks, just spoken of, he is speaking only of "the landmarks of the lectures," and adds—obviously referring to the sense in which we are now using the term—that there are other landmarks in the ancient institution of Freemasonry which have remained untouched in that publication, and it is not unanimously agreed to what they may be confined.

Next (1856) occurred the publication of Dr. Mackey's epoch-making exposition of the term and his well-known formulation of twenty-five landmarks. I shall return to these in another connection. But it is interesting to see the effect of this upon Oliver. In 1863, in his *Freemason's Treasury*, Oliver classifies the "Genuine Landmarks of Freemasonry" into twelve classes, of which he enumerates some forty existing, and about a dozen others as obsolete (nota bene) or as spurious. But he admits that we "are groveling in darkness" on the whole subject, and that "we have no actual criterion by which we may determine what is a landmark and what not." Nevertheless, Oliver's ideas were beginning to be fixed, as a result of Mackey's exposition, and it is significant that in 1862, Stephen Barton Wilson, a well-known English Masonic preceptor of that time, published an article in the *Freemason's Magazine* entitled *The Necessity of Maintaining the Ancient Landmarks of the Order* in which he takes landmarks to mean those laws of the Craft which are universal and irrevocable — the very sense which Mackey had adopted. After this, Mackey's definition of a landmark, his criteria of a landmark, and his exposition of the twenty-five landmarks obtained for a time universal acceptance. The whole was reprinted without comment in England in 1877 in Mackenzie's *Royal Masonic Cyclopaedia*. In 1878, Rev. Bro. Woodford, one of the best of the Masonic scholars of the time, questioned the details of Mackey's list, but without questioning his definition or his criteria. In the same way Lockwood, accepting the definition and the criteria, reduced Mackey's list of twenty-five to nineteen.

Presently Masonic scholars reopened the whole subject. Today three radically different views obtain. The first I should call the legal theory, the second the historical, theory, the third the philosophical theory. The legal theory accepts Mackey's idea of a body of universal unalterable fundamental principles which are at the foundation of all Masonic law. But the tendency has been to reduce Mackey's list very considerably, although two of our jurisdictions greatly extend it. Nine American Grand Lodges tell us that the old charges contain the ancient landmarks. Seven Grand Lodges have adopted statements of their own, varying from the seven of West Virginia and the noteworthy ten of New Jersey to the thirty-nine of Nevada and fifty-four of Kentucky. These declaratory enactments — exactly analogous to attempts to reduce the fundamental rights of man to chapter and verse in the bills of rights in American constitutions — are highly significant for the study of Masonic common law, and deserve to be examined critically by one who would know the received doctrines of the traditional element in the Masonic legal system. But since the admirable report in New Jersey in 1903 and the careful examination of Mackey's list by Bro. George F. Moore in his papers in the *New Age* in 1910-12, it is quite futile to contend for the elaborate formulations which are still so common. If, however, we distinguish between the landmarks and the common law, we may still believe that there are landmarks in Mackey's sense and may hope to formulate them as far as fundamental principles may be formulated in any organic institution.

The historical theory, proceeding upon the use of the word landmark in our books, denies that there is such a thing as the legal theory assumes. The skeptic says, first, that down to the appearance of Mackey's *Masonic Jurisprudence* "landmark" was a term floating about in Masonic writing without any definite meaning. It had come down from the operative Craft where it had meant trade secrets, and had been used loosely for "traditions" or for "authorized ritual" or for "significant historical occurrences," and Oliver had even talked of "obsolete landmarks." Second, he says, the definition of a landmark, the criteria of a landmark, and the fixed landmarks generally received in England and America from 1860 on, come from Mackey.

Granting the force of the skeptic's argument, however, it does not seem to me that the essential achievement of Mackey's book is overthrown. I have already shown that a notion of unalterable, fundamental principles and groundwork and of a "body of Masonry" beyond the reach of innovation can be traced from the revival to the present. This is the important point. To seize upon the term landmark, floating about in Masonic literature, and apply it to this fundamental law was a happy stroke. Even if landmark had meant many other things, there was warrant for this use in Payne's *Regulations*, the name was an apt one, and the institution was a reality in Masonry, whatever its name. The second theory seems to me to go too much upon the use of the word landmark and not enough upon the thing itself.

Under the influence of the second theory, and in a laudable desire to save a useful word, a philosophical theory has been urged which applies the term to a few fundamental ethical or philosophical or religious tenets which may he put at the basis of the Masonic institution.

Thus, Bro. Newton in a note to the valuable paper of Bro. Shepherd in volume one of *The Builder*, proposes as a statement of the landmarks: "The fatherhood of God, the brotherhood of man, the moral law, the Golden Rule, and the hope of a life everlasting."

This is admirable of its kind. The Masonic lawyer, however, must call for some legal propositions. Either we have a fundamental law, or we have not. If we have, whether it be called the landmarks or something else is no great matter. But the settled usage of England and America since Mackey wrote ought to be decisive so long as no other meaning of the term can make a better title.

Next then, let us take up Mackey's theory of the landmarks, and first his definition. He says the landmarks are "those ancient and universal customs of the order, which either gradually grew into operation as rules of action, or if at once enacted by any competent authority, were enacted at a period so remote that no account of their origin is to be found in the records of history. Both the enactors and the time of the enactment have passed away from the record, and the landmarks are therefore of higher authority than memory or history can reach." In reading this we must bear in mind that it was written in 1856, before the rise of modern Masonic history and before the rise of modern ideas in legal science in the United States. Hence it is influenced by certain uncritical ideas of Masonic history and by some ideas as to the making of customary law reminiscent of Hale's *History of the Common Law*, to which some lawyer may have directly or indirectly referred him. But we may reject these incidental points and the essential theory will remain unaffected — the theory of a body of immemorially recognized fundamentals which give to the Masonic order, if one may say so, its Masonic character, and may not be altered without taking away that character. It is true Mackey's list of landmarks goes beyond this. But it goes beyond his definition as he puts it; and the reason is to be found in his failure to distinguish between the landmarks and the common law.

Next Mackey lays down three requisites or characteristics of a landmark — (1) immemorial antiquity; (2) universality; (3) absolute irrevocability and immutability. He says; "It must have existed from time whereof the memory of man runneth not to the contrary. Its antiquity is an essential element. Were it possible for all the Masonic authorities at the present day to unite in one universal congress and with the most perfect unanimity to adopt any new regulation, although such regulation would while it remained unrepealed be obligatory on the whole Craft, yet it would not be a landmark. It would have the character of universality, it is true, but it would be wanting in that of antiquity." As to the third point, he says: "As the congress to which I have just alluded would not have the power to enact a landmark, so neither would it have the prerogative of abolishing one. The landmarks of the order, like the laws of the Medes and the Persians, can suffer no change. What they were centuries ago, they still remain and must so continue in force till Masonry itself shall cease to exist."

Let me pause here to suggest a point to the skeptics — for though I am not one of them, I think we must recognize the full force of their case. The point as to the regulation unanimously adopted by the universal Masonic congress is palpably taken from one of the stock illustrations of American law books. The legal futility of a petition of all the electors unanimously praying for a law counter to the constitution or of a resolution of a meeting of all the electors unanimously proclaiming such a law is a familiar proposition to the American constitutional lawyer. One cannot doubt that Mackey had in mind the analogy of our American legal and political institutions. Yet to show this by no means refutes Mackey's theory of a fundamental Masonic law. The idea of an unwritten fundamental law existing from time immemorial is characteristic of the Middle Ages and in another form prevailed in English thought at the time of the Masonic revival. To the Germanic peoples who came into western Europe and founded our modern states, the Roman idea of law as the will of the sovereign was wholly alien. They thought of law as something above human control, and of law-making as a search for the justice and truth of the Creator. In the words of Bracton, the king ruled under God and the law. To Coke in the seventeenth century even Parliament was under the law so that if it were to enact a statute "against common right and reason, or repugnant, or impossible to be performed" the common law would hold that statute void. In the reign of Henry VII, the English Court of Common Pleas actually did hold a statute void which attempted to make the king a parson without the consent of the head of the church and thus interfered with the fundamental distinction between the spiritual and the temporal. In 1701, Lord Holt, Lord Chief Justice of England, repeated Coke's doctrine and asserted that there were limitations upon the power of Parliament founded on natural principles of right and justice. This idea took form in America in our bills of rights and our constitutional law.

But it is not at all distinctively American. On the contrary the accidents of legal history preserved and developed the English medieval idea with us although it died in the eighteenth century at home. In the whole period of Masonry in England prior to the revival and in the formative period after the revival, this idea of an unwritten, immemorial fundamental law would have been accepted in any connection in which men spoke or thought of law at all.

For myself, I should recognize seven landmarks, which might be put summarily as follows: (1) Belief in God; (2) belief in the persistence of personality; (3) a "book of the law" as an indispensable part of the furniture of every lodge; (4) the legend of the third degree; (5) secrecy; (6) the symbolism of the operative art; and (7) that a Mason must be a man, free born, and of age. Two more might be added, namely, the government of the lodge by master and wardens and the right of a Mason in good standing to visit. But these seem doubtful to me, and doubt is a sufficient warrant for referring them to the category of common law.

"Belief in God, the G. A. O. T. U.," says Bro. Moore, "is the first landmark of Freemasonry." Doubtless Mackey would have agreed, though in his list it bears the number nineteen. For this landmark we may vouch:

(1) The testimony of the old charges in which invariably and from the very beginning there is the injunction to be true to God and holy church. Anderson's change, which produced so much dispute, was directed to the latter clause. As the medieval church was taken to be universal, the addition was natural. In eighteenth-century England there was a manifest difficulty. But the idea of God is universal and there seems no warrant for rejecting the whole of the ancient injunction.

(2) The resolution of the Grand Lodge of England that the Master Mason's obligation contains the ancient landmarks.

(3) The religious character of primitive secret societies and all societies and fraternities founded thereon.

(4) The consensus of Masonic philosophers as to the objects and purposes of the fraternity.

(5) The consensus of Anglo-American Masons, in the wake of the Grand Lodge of England, in ceasing to recognize the Grand Orient of France after the change in its constitutions made in 1877.

The second landmark, as I have put them, is number twenty in Mackey's list. He says: "Subsidiary to this belief in God, as a landmark of the order, is the belief in a resurrection to a future life. This landmark is not so positively impressed in the candidate by exact words as the preceding; but the doctrine is taught by very plain implication and runs through the whole symbolism of the order. To believe in Masonry and not to believe in a resurrection would be an absurd anomaly, which could only be excused by the reflection that he who thus confounded his skepticism was so ignorant of the meaning of both theories as to have no foundation for his knowledge of either."

Perhaps Mackey's meaning here is less dogmatic than his words. Perhaps any religious doctrine of persistence of personality after death would satisfy his true meaning, so that the Buddhist doctrine of transmigration and ultimate Nirvana would meet Masonic requirements. Certainly, it is true that our whole symbolism from the entrance naked and defenseless to the legend of the third degree is based on this idea of persistence of personality. Moreover, this same symbolism is universal in ancient rites and primitive secret societies. True in the most primitive ones it signifies only the passing of the child and the birth of the man. Yet even here the symbolism is significant. I see no reason to reject this landmark.

We come now to an alleged landmark about which a great controversy still rages. I have put it third. In Mackey's list it is number twenty-one. I will first give Mackey's own words: "It is a landmark that a 'book of the law' shall constitute an indispensable part of the furniture of every lodge. I say advisedly book of the law because it is not absolutely required that everywhere the old and new testament shall be used. The book of the law is that volume which, by the religion of the country, is believed to contain the revealed will of the Grand Architect of the Universe. Hence in all lodges in Christian countries, the book of the law is composed of the old and new testaments. In a country where Judaism was the prevailing faith, the old testament alone would be sufficient; and in Mohammedan countries and among Mohammedan Masons, the Koran might be substituted."

Perhaps the point most open to criticism here is that it must be the book accepted as the word of God by the religion of the country. For example, in India, lodges in which Englishmen sit with Hindus and Mohammedans, keep the Bible, the Koran and the Shasters among the lodge furniture, and obligate the initiate upon the book of his faith.

The essential idea here seems to be that Masonry is, if not a religious institution, at least an institution which recognizes religion and seeks to be a co-worker with it toward moral progress of mankind. Hence it keeps as a part of its furniture the book of the law which is the visible and tangible evidence of the Mason's adherence to religion. In so doing we are confirmed by the evidence of primitive secret societies; for religion, morals, law, church, public opinion, government were all united in these societies at first and gradually differentiated. The relation of Masonry with religion, in its origin, in its whole history, and in its purposes, is so close that there is a heavy burden of proof on those who seek to reject this tangible sign of the relation, which stood unchallenged in universal Masonic usage till the Grand Orient of France in 1877 substituted the book of Masonic constitutions. In view of the universal protest which that action brought forth, of the manifest impossibility of accepting the French resolution as fixing the ends of the order, of the uniform practice of obligating Masons on the book of the law, as far back as we know Masonry, and as shown uniformly in the old charges, it seems impossible not to accept Mackey's twenty-first landmark in the sense of having a recognized book or books of religion among the furniture of the lodge and obligating candidates thereon. Indeed, the English Grand-Lodge resolution that the Master Mason's obligation includes the landmarks of Masonry, seems fairly to include the taking of that obligation upon the book of the law, as it was then taken.

Fourth I have put the legend of the third degree. This is Mackey's third landmark. "Any rite," he says, "which should exclude it or materially alter it, would at once by that exclusion or alteration cease to be a Masonic rite." Here certainly we have something that meets the criteria of immemorial antiquity and of universality. The symbolism of resurrection is to be found in all primitive secret rites and in all the rites of antiquity, and the ceremony of death and re-birth is one of the oldest of human institutions.

Fifth I have put secrecy. Mackey develops this in his eleventh and twenty-third landmarks. The exact limits must be discussed in another connection. But if anything in Masonry is immemorial and universal and if the testimony of ancient and primitive rites counts for anything at all, we may at least set up the requirement of secrecy as an unquestioned landmark.

Sixth I should recognize as a landmark employment of the symbolism of the operative art. This is Mackey's twenty-fourth landmark. Perhaps one might say that it is a fundamental tenet of Masonry that we are Masons. But it is worthy of notice that this symbolism is significantly general in ancient and primitive teaching through secret rites.

Finally, I should put it as a landmark that the Mason must be a man, free born, and of full age according to the law or custom of the time and place. This is in part Mackey's eighteenth landmark, though he goes further and requires that the man be whole. I shall discuss the latter requirements in connection with Masonic common law. As to the form for which I contend, perhaps I need only vouch (1) the vote of the Grand Lodge of England that the Master Mason's obligation contains the landmarks; (2) universal, immemorial and unquestioned usage; and (3) the men's house of primitive society and its derivatives.

A special question may possibly arise in connection with the proposition that it is a landmark that no woman shall be made a Mason. No doubt all of you have heard of the famous case of Miss St. Leger, or as she afterwards became, the Hon. Mrs. Aldworth, the so-called woman Mason. Pictures of this eminent sister in Masonic costume, labeled "The Woman Mason" are not uncommon in our books. The initiating of Mrs. Aldworth is alleged to have taken place in 1735 in lodge No. 44 at Doneraile in Ireland. She was the sister of Viscount Doneraile who was Master, and as the lodge met usually at his residence, Doneraile House, the story is she made a hole in the brick wall of the room with scissors and so watched the first and second degrees from an adjoining room. At this point she fell from her perch and so was discovered. After much debate, so the story goes, the Entered Apprentice and Fellowcraft obligations were given her. This transaction was first made known in a memoir published in 1807 — seventy-two years afterwards. Modern English Masonic historians have examined the story critically and have proved beyond question that it must be put among the Masonic apocrypha. The proof is too long to go into here, where in any event it is a digression. But I may refer you to Gould's larger work where you will find it in full.

Of course, the action of a single lodge in 1735 would not be conclusive-against (1) the terms of the Master Mason's obligation; (2) the resolution of the Grand Lodge of England in the eighteenth century; (3) the weighty circumstances that all secret societies of primitive man and the societies among all peoples in all times that continue the tradition of the men's house were exclusively societies of men. But it is after all a relief in these days of militant feminism, to know that we are not embarrassed by any precedent.

Such are the landmarks as I conceive them. But much remains to be said about other institutions or doctrines which have some claim to stand in this category when we come next to consider Masonic common law.

Appendix E

THE
CHARGES
OF A
FREE-MASON,

EXTRACTED FROM
The Ancient RECORDS of LODGES
beyond Sea, and of those in England, Scotland,
and Ireland, for the Use of the Lodges in LONDON:
TO BE READ
At The Making of NEW BRETHREN, or when the
MASTER shall order it.

The General Heads, VIZ
I. Of GOD and RELIGION.
II. Of the CIVIL MAGISTRATES, supreme and subordinate.
III. Of LODGES.
IV. Of MASTERS, Wardens, Fellows, and Apprentices.
V. Of the Management of the Craft in working.
VI. Of BEHAVIOUR, viz.
   1. In the Lodge while constituted.
   2. After the Lodge is over and the Brethren not gone.
   3. When Brethren meet without Strangers, but not in a Lodge.
   4. In Presence of Strangers not Masons.
   5. At Home and in the Neighborhood.
   6. Towards a strange Brother.

I. Concerning GOD and RELIGION.

A Mason is oblig'd by his Tenure, to obey the moral Law; and if he rightly understands the Art, he will never be a stupid Atheist nor an irreligious Libertine. But though in ancient Times Masons were charg'd in every Country to be of the Religion of that Country or Nation, whatever it was, yet 'tis now thought more expedient only to oblige them to that Religion in which all Men agree, leaving their particular Opinions to themselves; that is, to be good Men and true, or Men of Honor and Honesty, by whatever Denominations or Persuasions they may be distinguish'd; whereby Masonry becomes the Center of Union, and the Means of conciliating true Friendship among Persons that must have remain'd at a perpetual Distance.

II. Of the CIVIL MAGISTRATES supreme and subordinate.

A Mason is a peaceable Subject to the Civil Powers, wherever he resides or works, and is never to be concern'd in Plots and Conspiracies against the Peace and Welfare of the Nation, nor to behave himself undutifully to inferior Magistrates; for as Masonry hath been always injured by War, Bloodshed, and Confusion, so ancient Kings and Princes have been much dispos'd to encourage the Craftsmen, because of their Peaceableness and Loyalty, whereby they practically answer'd the Cavils of their Adversaries, and promoted the Honour of the Fraternity, whoever flourish'd in Times of Peace. So that if a Brother should be a Rebel against the State, he is not to be countenanc'd in his Rebellion, however he may be pitied as an unhappy Man; and, if convicted of no other Crime though the loyal Brotherhood must and ought to disown his Rebellion, and give no Umbrage or Ground of political Jealousy to the Government for the time being; they cannot expel him from the Lodge, and his Relation to it remains indefeasible.

III. Of LODGES.

A LODGE is a place where Masons assemble and work: Hence that Assembly, or duly organiz'd Society of Masons, is call'd a LODGE, and every Brother ought to belong to one, and to be subject to its By-Laws and the GENERAL REGULATIONS. It is either particular or general, and will be best understood by attending it, and by the Regulations of the General or Grand Lodge hereunto annex'd. In ancient Times, no Master or Fellow could be absent from it especially when warn'd to appear at it, without incurring a sever Censure, until it appear'd to the Master and Wardens that pure Necessity hinder'd him.

The persons admitted Members of a Lodge must be good and true Men, free-born, and of mature and discreet Age, no Bondmen no Women, no immoral or scandalous men, but of good Report.

IV. Of Masters, WARDENS, Fellows and Apprentices.

All preferment among Masons is grounded upon real Worth and personal Merit only; that so the Lords may be well served, the Brethren not put to Shame, nor the Royal Craft despis'd: Therefore, no Master or Warden is chosen by Seniority, but for his Merit. It is impossible to describe these things in Writing, and every Brother must attend in his Place, and learn them in a way peculiar to this Fraternity: Only Candidates may know that no Master should take an Apprentice unless he has sufficient Employment for him, and unless he be a perfect Youth having no Maim or Defect in his

Body that may render him uncapable of learning the Art of serving his Master's LORD, and of being made a Brother, and then a Fellow-Craft in due time, even after he has served such a Term of Years as the Custom of the Country directs; and that he should be descended of honest Parents; that so, when otherwise qualify'd he may arrive to the Honour of being the WARDEN, and then the Master of the Lodge, the Grand Warden, and at length the GRAND MASTER of all the Lodges, according to his Merit.

No Brother can be a WARDEN until he has pass'd the part of a Fellow-Craft; nor a MASTER until he has acted as a Warden, nor GRAND WARDEN until he has been Master of a Lodge, nor Grand Master unless he has been a Fellow-Craft before his Election, who is also to be nobly born, or a Gentleman of the best Fashion, or some eminent Scholar, or some curious Architect, or other Artist, descended of honest Parents, and who is of similar great Merit in the Opinion of the Lodges. And for the better, and easier, and more honourable Discharge of his Office, the Grand-Master has a Power to chuse his own DEPUTY GRAND-MASTER, who must be then, or must have been formerly, the Master of a particular Lodge, and has the Privilege of acting whatever the GRAND MASTER, his Principal, should act, unless the said Principal be present, or interpose his Authority by a Letter

These Rulers and Governors, supreme and subordinate, of the ancient Lodge, are to be obey'd in their respective Stations by all the Brethren, according to the old Charges and Regulations, with all Humility, Reverence, Love and Alacrity.

V. Of the Management of the CRAFT in working.

All Masons shall work honestly on working Days, that they may live creditably on holy Days; and the time appointed by the Law of the Land or confirm'd by Custom, shall be observ'd.

The most expert of the Fellow-Craftsmen shall be chosen or appointed the Master or Overseer of the Lord's Work; who is to be call'd MASTER by those that work under him. The Craftsmen are to avoid all ill Language, and to call each other by no disobliging Name, but Brother or Fellow; and to behave themselves courteously within and without the Lodge. The Master, knowing himself to be able of Cunning, shall undertake the Lord's Work as reasonably as possible, and truly dispend his Goods as if they were his own; nor to give more Wages to any Brother or Apprentice than he really may deserve.

Both the Master and the Masons receiving their Wages justly, shall be faithful to the Lord and honestly finish their Work, whether Task or journey; nor put the work to Task that hath been accustomed to Journey.

None shall discover Envy at the Prosperity of a Brother, nor supplant him, or put him out of his Work, if he be capable to finish the same; for no

Man can finish another's Work so much to the Lord's Profit, unless he be thoroughly acquainted with the Designs and Draughts of him that began it.

When a Fellow-Craftsman is chosen Warden of the Work under the Master, he shall be true both to Master and Fellows, shall carefully oversee the Work in the Master's Absence to the Lord's profit; and his Brethren shall obey him.

All Masons employed shall meekly receive their Wages without Murmuring or Mutiny, and not desert the Master till the Work is finish'd.

A younger Brother shall be instructed in working, to prevent spoiling the Materials for want of Judgment, and for increasing and continuing of Brotherly Love.

All the Tools used in working shall be approved by the Grand Lodge.

No Labourer shall be employ'd in the proper Work of Masonry; nor shall Free Masons work with those that are not free, without an urgent Necessity; nor shall they teach Labourers and unaccepted Masons as they should teach a Brother or Fellow.

VI. Of BEHAVIOUR, VIZ.

1. In the Lodge while constituted.

You are not to hold private Committees, or separate Conversation without Leave from the Master, nor to talk of anything impertinent or unseemly, nor interrupt the Master or Wardens, or any Brother speaking to the Master: Nor behave yourself ludicrously or jestingly while the Lodge is engaged in what is serious and solemn; nor use any unbecoming Language upon any Pretense whatsoever; but to pay due Reverence to your Master, Wardens, and Fellows, and put them to worship.

If any Complaint be brought, the Brother found guilty shall stand to the Award and Determination of the Lodge, who are the proper and competent Judges of all such Controversies (unless you carry it by Appeal to the GRAND LODGE), and to whom they ought to be referr'd, unless a Lord's Work be hinder'd the meanwhile, in which Case a particular Reference may be made; but you must never go to Law about what concerneth Masonry, without an absolute necessity apparent to the Lodge.

2. Behaviour after the LODGE is over and the Brethren not gone.

You may enjoy yourself with innocent Mirth, treating one another according to Ability, but avoiding all Excess, or forcing any Brother to eat or drink beyond his Inclination, or hindering him from going when his Occasions call him, or doing or saying anything offensive, or that may forbid an easy and free Conversation, for that would blast our Harmony, and defeat our laudable Purposes. Therefore, no private Piques or Quarrels must be brought within the Door of the Lodge, far less any Quarrels about Religion, or Nations, or State Policy, we, being only as Masons of the

Catholick Religion above mention'd, we are also of all Nations, Tongues, Kindreds, and Languages, and are resolv'd against all Politics, as what never yet conduct'd to the Welfare of the Lodge, nor ever will. This Charge has been always strictly enjoin'd and observ'd; but especially ever since the Reformation in BRITAIN, or the Dissent and Secession of these Nations from the Communion of ROME.

3. Behaviour when Brethren meet without Strangers, but not in a Lodge form'd.

You are to salute one another in a courteous Manner, as you will be instructed, calling each other Brother, freely giving mutual instruction as shall be thought expedient, without being ever seen or overheard, and without encroaching upon each other, or derogating from that Respect which is due to any Brother, were he not Mason: For though all Masons are as Brethren upon the same Level, yet Masonry takes no Honour from a man that he had before; nay, rather it adds to his Honour, especially if he has deserv'd well of the Brotherhood, who must give Honour to whom it is due, and avoid ill Manners.

4. Behaviour in Presence of Strangers not Masons.

You shall be cautious in your Words and Carriage, that the most penetrating Stranger shall not be able to discover or find out what is not proper to be intimated, and sometimes you shall divert a Discourse, and manage it prudently for the Honour of the worshipful Fraternity.

5. Behaviour at Home, and in your Neighbourhood.

You are to act as becomes a moral and wise Man; particularly not to let your Family, Friends and Neighbors know the Concern of the Lodge, &c., but wisely to consult your own Honour, and that of the ancient Brotherhood, for reasons not to be mention'd here You must also consult your Health, by not continuing together too late, or too long from Home, after Lodge Hours are past; and by avoiding of Gluttony or Drunkenness, that your Families be not neglected or injured, nor you disabled from working.

6. Behaviour towards a strange Brother.

You are cautiously to examine him, in such a Method as Prudence shall direct you, that you may not be impos'd upon by an ignorant, false Pretender, whom you are to reject with Contempt and Derision, and beware of giving him any Hints of Knowledge.

But if you discover him to be a true and genuine Brother, you are to respect him accordingly; and if he is in want, you must relieve him if you can, or else direct him how he may be reliev'd: you must employ him some days, or else recommend him to be employ'd. But you are not charged to do beyond your Ability, only to prefer a poor Brother, that is a good Man and true before any other poor People in the same Circumstance.

Finally, All these Charges you are to observe, and also those that shall be recommended to you in another Way; cultivating BROTHERLY-LOVE, the Foundation and Cape-stone, the Cement and Glory of this Ancient Fraternity, avoiding all Wrangling and Quarreling, all Slander and Backbiting, nor permitting others to slander any honest Brother, but defending his Character, and doing him all good Offices, as far as is consistent with your Honour and Safety, and no farther. And if any of them do you Injury, you must apply to your own or his Lodge, and from thence you may appeal to the Grand Lodge, at the Quarterly Communication and from thence to the annual GRAND LODGE at the Quarterly Communication, and from thence to the annual GRAND LODGE, as has been the ancient laudable Conduct of our Fore-fathers in every Nation; never taking a legal Course but when the Case cannot be otherwise decided, and patiently listening to the honest and friendly Advice of Master and Fellows, when they would prevent your going to Law with Strangers, or would excite you to put a speedy Period to all Law-Suits, so that you may mind the Affair of MASONRY with the more Alacrity and Success; but with respect to Brothers or Fellows at Law, the Master and Brethren should kindly offer their Mediation, which ought to be thankfully submitted to by the contending Brethren; and if that submission is impracticable, they must, however, carry on their Process, or Law-Suit, without Wrath and Rancor (not in the common way) saying or doing nothing which may hinder Brotherly Love, and good Offices to be renew'd and continu'd; that all may see the benign Influence of MASONRY, as all true Masons have done from the beginning of the World, and will do to the End of Time.

Amen so mote it be.

Appendix F

Anderson's Constitutions of 1723

General Regulations,
Compiled first by MR. GEORGE PAYNE, Anno 1720, when he was Grand-Master, and approv'd by the Grand Lodge on St. John Baptist's Day, Anno 1721; at Stationer's Hall, London ; when the most noble PRINCE John, Duke of MONTAGU, was unanimously chosen our Grand Master for the Year ensuing; who chose JOHN BEAL, M.D., his Deputy GRAND MASTER ; and { Mr. Josiah Villeneau Mr. Thomas Morris, jun. } were chosen by the Lodge GRAND-WARDENS.

And now, by the Command of our said Right Worshipful GRAND-MASTER MONTAGU, the Author of this Book has compar'd them with, and reduc'd them to the ancient Records and immemorial Usage of the Fraternity, and digested them into this new Method, with several proper Explications for the Use of the Lodges in and about London and Westminster.

I. THE Grand Master or his DEPUTY hath Authority and Right, not only to be present in any true Lodge, but also to preside wherever he is, with the Master of the Lodge on his Left Hand, and to order his Grand-Wardens to attend him, who are not to act in particular Lodges as Wardens, but in his Presence, and at his Command ; because there the GRAND-MASTER may command the Wardens of that Lodge, or any other Brethren he pleaseth, to attend and act as his Wardens pro tempore.

II. THE MASTER of a particular Lodge, has the right and authority of congregating the Members of his Lodge into a Chapter at Pleasure, upon any Emergency or Occurrence as well as to appoint the time and place of their usual forming : And in case of Sickness Death, or necessary Absence of the MASTER, the Senior Warden shall act as Master pro tempore, if no Brother is present who has been Master of that Lodge before ; for in that Case the absent Master's Authority reverts to the last Master then present ; though he cannot act until the said senior Warden has once congregated the Lodge or in his Absence the junior Warden.

III. THE MASTER of each particular Lodge, or one of the Wardens, or some other Brother by his Order, shall keep a Book containing their By-Laws, the Names of their Members, with a list of all the Lodges in Town, and the usual Times and Places of their forming, and all their Transactions that are proper to be written

IV. No Lodge shall make more than FIVE new Brethren at one Time, nor any Man under the Age of Twenty-five, who must be also his own Master; unless by a Dispensation from the Grand Master or his Deputy.

V. No man can be made or admitted a Member of a particular Lodge, without previous Notice one Month before given to the said Lodge, in order to make due Inquiry into the Reputation and Capacity of the Candidate; unless by the Dispensation aforesaid.

VI. But no man can be enter'd a Brother in any particular Lodge, or admitted to be a Member thereof, without the unanimous Consent of all the Members of that Lodge then present when the Candidate is propos'd, and their Consent is formally askd by the Master; and they are to signify their Consent or Dissent in their own Prudent Way, either virtually or in form, but with Unanimity: Nor is this inherent Privilege subject to a Dispensation; because the Members of a particular Lodge are the best Judges of it; and if a fractious Member should be impos'd on them, it might spoil their Harmony, or hinder their Freedom; or even break and disperse the Lodge, which ought to be avoided by all good and true Brethren.

VII. Every new Brother at his making is recently to cloath the Lodge, that is, all the Brethren present, and to deposit something for the Relief of indigent and decay'd Brethren, as the Candidate shall think fit to bestow, over and above the small allowance stated by the By-Laws of that particular Lodge, which Charity shall be lodgd with the Master or Wardens, or the Cashier, if the Members see fit to chuse one.

And the Candidate shall also solemnly promise to submit to the Constitution, the Charges and Regulations, and to such other good Usages as shall be intimated to them in Time and Place convenient.

VIII. No set or Number of Brethren shall withdraw or separate themselves from the Lodge in which they were made Brethren, or were afterwards admitted Members, unless the Lodge becomes too numerous; nor even then, without a Dispensation from the Grand Master or his Deputy; and when they are thus separated, they must either immediately join themselves to such other Lodge as they shall like best, with the unanimous Consent of that other Lodge to which they go (as above regulated), or else they must obtain the Grand Master's Warrant to join in forming a new Lodge.

If any set or Number of Masons shall take upon themselves to form a Lodge without the Grand Master's Warrant, the regular Lodges are not to countenance them, or own them as fair brethren and duly form'd, nor approve of their Acts and Deeds; but must treat them as Rebels, until they humble themselves, as the Grand Master, shall, in his Prudence, direct, and until he approve of them by his Warrant, which must be signified to the other Lodges, as the Custom is when a new Lodge is to be registered in the List of Lodges.

IX. But if any Brother so far misbehave himself as to render his Lodge uneasy, he shall be twice duly admonished by the Master or Wardens in a form'd Lodge; and if he will not refrain his Imprudence, and obediently submit to the Advice of the Brethren, and reform what gives them Offense, he shall be dealt with according to the By-Laws of that particular Lodge, or else in such a manner as the Quarterly Communication shall in their great prudence think fit; for which a new Regulation may be afterward made.

X. The Majority of every particular Lodge, when congregated, shall have the Privilege of giving Instructions to their Masters and Wardens before the assembling of the Grand Chapter or Lodge, at the three Quarterly Communications hereafter mention'd and of the annual Grand Lodge, too; because their Master and Wardens are their Representatives, and are supposed to speak their mind.

XI. All particular Lodges are to observe the same usages as much as possible; in order to which, and for cultivating a good Understanding among Free-Masons, some members out of every Lodge shall be deputed to visit the other Lodges as often as shall be thought convenient.

XII. The Grand Lodge consists of, and is form'd by, the Masters and Wardens of all the regular particular Lodges upon Record, with the Grand Master at their Head, and his Deputy on his Left hand, and the Grand Wardens in their proper places; and must have a Quarterly Communication about Michaelmas, Christmas and Lady Day, in some convenient Place, as the Grand Master shall appoint, where no Brother shall be present, who is not at that time a Member thereof, without a Dispensation; and while he stays, he shall not be allow'd to vote, nor even given his Opinion without Leave of the Grand Lodge askd and given, or unless it be duly askd by the said Lodge.

All matters are to be determined in the Grand Lodge by a Majority of Votes, each member having one Vote, and the Grand Master having two Votes, unless the said Lodge leave any particular thing to the Determination of the Grand Master for the sake of Expedition.

XIII. At the said Quarterly Communication all Masters that concern the Fraternity in general, or particular Lodges, or single Brethren, are quietly, sedately and maturely to be discoursed and transacted; Apprentices must be admitted Masters and Fellow-Craft only here, unless by a Dispensation. Here also all differences, that cannot be made up and accommodated privately, nor by a particular Lodge, are to be seriously considered and decided: And if any Brother thinks himself aggrieved by the Decision of this Board, he may Appeal to the annual Grand Lodge next ensuing, and leave his Appeal in Writing with the Grand Master, or his Deputy, or the Grand Wardens.

Here also the Master or the Wardens of each particular Lodge shall bring and produce a List of such Members as have been made or even admitted in their particular Lodges since the last Communication of the Grand Lodge. And there shall be a book kept by the Grand Master, or his Deputy, or rather by some Brother whom the Grand Lodge shall appoint for Secretary, wherein shall be recorded all the Lodges, with their usual Times and Places of forming, and the Names of all the Members of each Lodge; and all the Affairs of the Grand Lodge that are proper to be written.

They shall also consider of the most prudent and effectual Methods of collecting and disposing of what Money shall be given to, or Lodged with them in Charity, towards the Relief only of any true Brother fallen into poverty or Decay, but of no one else. But every particular Lodge shall dispose of their own Charity for poor Brethren, according to their own By-Laws, until it be agreed by all the Lodges (in a new Regulation) to carry in the Charity collection by them to the Grand Lodge, at the Quarterly or Annual Communication, in order to make a common Stock of it, for the more handsome Relief of poor Brethren.

They shall appoint a Treasurer, a Brother of good worldly Substance, who shall be a Member of the Grand Lodge by virtue of his Office, and shall be always present, and have Power to move to the Grand Lodge anything, especially what concerns his Office. To him shall be committed all Money rais'd for Charity, or for any other Use of the Grand Lodge, which he shall write down in a book, with the respective Ends and Uses for which the several Sums are intended; and shall expend or disburse the same by such a certain Order sign'd, as the Grand Lodge shall afterwards agree to in a new Regulation: But he shall not vote in chusing a Grand Master or Wardens, though in every other Transaction. As in like manner the Secretary shall be a Member of the Grand Lodge by virtue of his Office, and vote in everything except in chusing a Grand Master or Wardens.

The Treasurer and Secretary shall have each a Clerk, who must be a Brother and Fellow-Craft, but never must be a member of the Grand Lodge, nor speak without being allow'd or desir'd.

The Grand Master or his Deputy, shall always command the Treasurer and Secretary, with their Clerks and Books in order to see how Matters go on, and to know what is expedient to be done upon any emergent Occasion.

Another Brother (who must be a Fellow-Craft) should be appointed to look after the Door of the Grand Lodge; but shall be no member of it.

But these Officers may be farther explain'd by a new Regulation, when the Necessity and Expediency of them may more appear than at present to the Fraternity.

XIV. If at any Grand Lodge, stated or occasional, quarterly or annual, the Grand Master and his Deputy should be both absent, then the present Master of a Lodge, that has been the longest a Free Mason, shall take the Chair, and preside as Grand Master pro tempore; and shall be vested with all his Power and Honour for the time; provided there is no Brother present that has been Grand Master formerly, or Deputy Grand Master; for the last Grand Master present, or else the last Deputy present, should always of right take place in the Absence of the present Grand Master and his Deputy.

XV. In the Grand Lodge none can act as Wardens but the Grand Wardens themselves, if present; and if absent, the Grand Master, or the Person who presides in his place, shall order private Wardens to act as Grand Wardens pro tempore, whose Places are to be supplid by two Fellow-Craft of the same Lodge, calld forth to act, or sent thither by the particular Master thereof; or if by him omitted, then they shall be calld by the Grand Master, that so the Grand Lodge may be always complete.

XVI. The Grand Wardens, or any others, are first to advise with the Deputy about the Affairs of the Lodge or of the Brethren, and not to apply to the Grand Master without the knowledge of the Deputy, unless he refuse his Concurrence in any certain necessary affair; in which Case, or in case of any Difference between the Deputy and the Grand Wardens or other Brethren both parties are to go by Concert to the Grand Master, who can easily decide the Controversy and make up the Difference by virtue of his great Authority.

The Grand Master should receive no Intimation of Business concerning Masonry, but from his Deputy first, except in such certain Cases as his Worship can well judge of; for if the Application the Grand Master be irregular, he can easily order the Grand Wardens or any other Brethren thus applying, to wait upon his Deputy, who is to prepare the Business speedily, and to lay it orderly before his Worship.

XVII. No Grand Master, Deputy Grand Master, Grand Wardens, Treasurer, Secretary, or whoever acts for them, or in their stead pro tempore, can at the same time be the Master or Warden of a particular Lodge; but as soon as any of them has honorably dischargd his Grand Office, he returns to that post or station in his particular Lodge, from which he was calld to officiate above.

XVIII. If the Deputy Grand Master be sick, or necessarily absent, the Grand Master may chuse any Fellow-Craft he pleases to be his Deputy pro tempore: But he that is chosen Deputy at the Grand Lodge, and the Grand Wardens, too, cannot be discharged without the Cause fairly appear to the Majority of the Grand Lodge; and the Grand Master, if he is uneasy, may call a Grand Lodge on purpose to lay the Case before them, and to have their Advice and Concurrence. In which case the Majority of the Grand Lodge, if they cannot reconcile the Master and his Deputy or his Wardens, are to concur in allowing the Master to discharge his said Deputy or his said Wardens, and to chuse another Deputy immediately; and the said Grand Lodge shall chuse other Wardens in that Case, that Harmony and Peace may be preserved.

XIX. If the Grand Master should abuse his Power, and render himself unworthy of the Obedience and Subjection of the Lodges, he shall be treated in a way and manner to be agreed upon in a new Regulation; because hitherto the ancient Fraternity have had no occasion for it, their former Grand Masters having all behaved themselves worthy of that honorable Office.

XX. The Grand Master, with his Deputy and Wardens, shall (at least once) go around and visit all the Lodges about Town during his Mastership.

XXI. If the Grand Master die during his Mastership, or by Sickness, or by Being beyond Sea, or any other way should be renderd uncapable of discharging his Office, the Deputy, in his Absence, the Senior Grand Warden, or in his Absence, the Junior, or in his Absence any three present Masters of Lodges, shall join to congregate the Grand Lodge immediately, to advise together upon that Emergency, and to send two of their Number to invite the last Grand Master to resume his office, which now in course reverts to him; or if he refuse, then the next last, and so backward: But if no former Grand Master can be found, then the Deputy shall act as Principal until another is chosen; or if there be no Deputy, then the oldest Master.

XXII. The Brethren of all the Lodges in and about London and Westminster, shall meet at an Annual Communication and Feast, in some convenient place, on St. John Baptist's Day, or else on St. John Evangelist's Day, as the Grand Lodge shall think fit by a new Regulation, having of late Years met on St. John Baptist's Day. Provided, The Majority of the Masters and Wardens with the Grand Master, his Deputy and Wardens, agree at their Quarterly Communication, three months before, that there shall be a Feast, and a General Communication of all Brethren: For if either the Grand Master, or the Majority of the particular Masters, are against it, it must be dropt for that Time.

But whether there shall be a Feast for all the Brethren, or not, yet the Grand Lodge must meet in some convenient Place annually on St. John's Day; or if it be Sunday, then on the next Day, in order to chuse every Year a new Grand Master, Deputy and Warden.

XXIII. If it be thought expedient, and the Grand Master, with the Majority of the Masters and Wardens, agree to hold a Grand Feast according to the ancient laudable Custom of Masons, then the Grand Wardens shall have the care of preparing the Tickets, seald with the Grand Master's Seal, of disposing of the Tickets, of receiving the money for the Tickets, of buying the Materials of the Feast, of finding out a proper and convenient Place to feast in; and of every other thing that concerns the Entertainment.

But that the Work may not be too burthensome to the two Grand Wardens, and that all Matters may be expeditiously and safely managed, the Grand Master or his Deputy shall have power to nominate and appoint a certain Number of Stewards, as his Worship shall think fit, to act in concert with the two Grand Wardens; all things relating to the Feast being decided among them by a Majority of Voices; except the Grand Master or his Deputy interpose by a particular Direction of Appointment.

XXIV. The Wardens and Stewards shall, in due time, wait upon the Grand Master or his Deputy for Directions and Orders about the Premises; but if his Worship and his Deputy are sick, or necessarily absent, they shall call together the Masters and Wardens of Lodges to meet on purpose for their Advice and Orders; or else they may take the Matter wholly upon themselves and do the best they can.

The Grand Wardens and the Stewards are to account for all the Money they receive, or expend, to the Grand Lodge, after dinner, or when the Grand Lodge shall think fit to receive their Accounts.

If the Grand Master pleases, he may in due time summons all the Masters and Wardens of Lodges to consult with them about ordering the Grand Feast, and about any Emergency or accidental thing relating thereunto, that may require Advice; or else to take it upon himself altogether.

XXV. The Masters of Lodges shall each appoint one experienced and discreet Fellow-Craft of his Lodge, to compose a Committee, consisting of one from every Lodge, who shall meet to receive, in a convenient Apartment, every Person that brings a Ticket, and shall have Power to discourse him, if they think fit, in order to admit him or debar him, as they shall see cause; Provided they send no Man away before they have acquainted all the Brethren within Doors with the Reasons thereof, to avoid Mistakes, that so no true Brother may be debarr'd, nor a false Brother, or more Pretender, admitted. This Committee must meet very early on St. John's Day at the Place, even before any Person come with Tickets.

XXVI. The Grand Master shall appoint two or more trusty Brethren to be Porters or Door-Keepers, who are also to be early at the Place, for some good Reasons; and who are to be at the Command of the Committee.

XXVII. The Grand Wardens, or the Stewards, shall appoint beforehand such a Number of Brethren to serve at Table as they think fit and proper for that Work; and they may advise with the Masters and Wardens of Lodges about the most proper Persons, if they please, or may take in such by their Recommendation; for none are to serve that Day but free and accepted Masons, that the Communication may be free and harmonious.

XXVIII. All the Members of the Grand Lodge must be at the Place long before Dinner, with the Grand Master or his Deputy at their Head, who shall retire and form themselves. And this is done in order:

1. To receive any Appeals duly lodgd, as above regulated, that the appellant may be heard, and the Affair may be amicably decided before Dinner, if possible; but if it cannot, it must be delay'd till after the new Grand Master is elected; and if it cannot be decided after Dinner, it may be delay'd and referr'd to a particular Committee, that shall quietly adjust it, and make Report to the next Quarterly Communication, that Brotherly Love may be preserved.

2. To prevent any Difference or Disgust which may be feared to arise that Day; that no Interruption maybe given to the Harmony and Pleasure of the Grand Feast.

3. To consult about whatever concerns the Decency and Decorum of the Grand Assembly, and to prevent all Indecency and ill Manners, the Assembly being promiscuous.

4. To receive and consider of any good Motion, or any momentous and important Affair, that shall be brought from the particular Lodges, by their Representatives, the several Masters and Wardens.

XXIX. After these things are discuss'd, the Grand Master and his Deputy, the Grand Wardens, or the Stewards, the Secretary, the Treasurer, the Clerks, and every other Person shall withdraw, and leave the Masters and Wardens of the Particular Lodges alone, in, order to consult amicably about electing a new Grand Master, or continuing the present, if they have not done it the Day before; and if they are unanimous for continuing the present Grand Master, his Worship shall be calld in, and humbly desird to do the Fraternity the Honour of ruling them for the Year ensuing. And after Dinner it will be known whether he accept of it or not: For it should not be discovered but by the Election itself.

XXX. Then the Master and Wardens and all the Brethren, may converse promiscuously, or as they please to sort together, until the Dinner is coming in, when every Brother takes his Seat at the Table.

XXXI. Sometime after Dinner the Grand Lodge is form'd, not in Retirement, but in the Presence of all the Brethren, who yet are not Members of it, and must not therefore speak until they are desird and allowed.

XXXII. If the Grand Master of last Year has consented with the Masters and Wardens in private, before Dinner, to continue for the Year ensuing; then one of the Grand Lodge, deputed for that Purpose, shall represent to all the Brethren his Worship's good Government, &c. And turning to him, shall, in the name of the Grand Lodge, humbly request him to do the Fraternity the great Honour (if nobly born, if not) the great Kindness, of continuing to be their Grand Master for the Year ensuing. And his Worship declaring his consent by a Bow or a Speech, as he pleases, the said deputed Member of the Grand Lodge shall proclaim him Grand Master, and all the Members of the Lodge shall salute him in due Form. And all the Brethren shall for a few minutes have leave to declare their Satisfaction, Pleasure and Congratulation.

XXXIII. But if either the Masters and Wardens have not in private, this Day before Dinner, nor the Day before, desird the last Grand Master to continue in the Mastership another Year, or if he, when desird, has not consented: Then,

The last Grand Master shall nominate his Successor for the year ensuing, who, if unanimously approv'd by the Grand Lodge and if there present, shall be proclaimd, saluted, and congratulated, the new Grand Master as above hinted, and immediately installed by the last Grand Master, according to Usage.

XXXIV. But if that Nomination is not unanimously approv'd, the new Grand Master shall be chosen immediately by Ballot, every Master and Warden writing his Man's name, and the last Grand Master writing his Man's Name too; and the Man whose name the last Grand Master shall first take out, casually or by chance, shall be Grand Master for the Year ensuing; and if present, he shall be proclaim'd, saluted, and congratulated, as above hinted, and forthwith installed by the last Grand Master, according to Usage.

XXXV. The last Grand Master thus continued, or the New Grand Master thus installed, shall next nominate and appoint his Deputy Grand Master, either the last or a new one, who shall be also declard, saluted, and congratulated as above hinted.

The Grand Master shall also nominate the new Grand Wardens, and if unanimously approv'd by the Grand Lodge, shall be declard, saluted, and congratulated, as above hinted; but if not, they shall be chosen by Ballot, in the same way as the Grand Master: And the Wardens of private Lodges are also to be chosen by Ballot in each Lodge, if the Members thereof do not agree to their Master's Nomination.

XXXVI. But If the Brother, whom the present Grand Master shall nominate for his Successor, or whom the Majority of the Grand Lodge shall happen to chuse by Ballot is, by sickness, or other necessary Occasion, absent from the Grand Feast, he cannot be proclaimed the New Grand Master, unless the old Grand Master, or some of the Masters and Wardens of the Grand Lodge can vouch, upon the Honour of a Brother, that the said Person, so nominated or chosen, will readily accept of the said Office; in which case the old Grand Master shall act as Proxy, and shall nominate the Deputy and Wardens in his Name, and in his name also receive the usual Honours. Homage, and Congratulation.

XXXVII. Then the Grand Master shall allow any Brother, Fellow-Craft, or Apprentice to speak, Directing his Discourse to his Worship; or to make any motion for the good of the Fraternity, which shall be either immediately considerd and finishd, or also referr'd to the Consideration of the Grand Lodge at their next communication, stated or occasional. When that is over.

XXXVIII. The Grand Master or his Deputy, or some Brother appointed by him, shall harangue all the Brethren, and give them good Advice: And lastly, after some other Transactions, that cannot be written in any language, the Brethren may go away or stay longer, as they please.

XXXIX. Every Annual Grand Lodge has an inherent Power and Authority to make new Regulations, or to alter these, for the real Benefits of this ancient Fraternity: Provided always that the old Land Marks be carefully preserved, and that such Alterations and new Regulations be proposed and agreed to at the third Quarterly Communication preceding the Annual Grand Feast, and that they be offered also to the Perusal of all the Brethren before Dinner, in writing, even of the youngest Apprentice, the Approbation and Consent of the Majority of all the Brethren present being absolutely necessary to make the same binding and obligatory; which must, after Dinner and after the new Grand Master is installd, be solemnly desird; as it was desird and obtained for these Regulations, when propos'd by the Grand Lodge, to about 150 Brethren on St. John Baptist's Day, 1721.